Nicholas Brady, Nahum Tate

A new version of the Psalms of David

fitted to the tunes used in churches

Nicholas Brady, Nahum Tate

A new version of the Psalms of David
fitted to the tunes used in churches

ISBN/EAN: 9783744767859

Printed in Europe, USA, Canada, Australia, Japan

Cover: Foto ©Lupo / pixelio.de

More available books at **www.hansebooks.com**

A New Version

OF THE

PSALMS

OF

DAVID,

FITTED TO THE

TUNES USED IN CHURCHES.

BY
N. BRADY, D.D.
Chaplain in Ordinary,

AND
N. TATE, Esq;
Poet-Laureat,

To HIS MAJESTY.

LONDON:

Printed for the
COMPANY of STATIONERS;

AND SOLD AT

STATIONERS-HALL, near LUDGATE-STREET,
And by most BOOKSELLERS.

MDCCXCVIII.

AT the Court at KENSINGTON,

DECEMBER the 3d, 1696.

PRESENT,

The KING's Most Excellent Majesty in
COUNCIL.

UPON the humble Petition of N. BRADY and N. TATE, this Day read at the Board, setting forth, That the Petitioners have, with the utmost Care and Industry, completed A New Version of the Psalms of David in English Metre, fitted for Publick Use; and humbly praying His Majesty's Royal Allowance, that the said Version may be used in such Congregations as think fit to receive it:

His Majesty, taking the same into His Royal Consideration, is pleased to order in Council, that the said New Version of the Psalms in English Metre be, and the same is hereby, Allowed and Permitted to be used in all such Churches, Chapels, and Congregations, as shall think fit to receive the same.

W. BRIDGMAN.

THE PSALMS OF DAVID.

PSALM I.

1 HOW bleft is he, who ne'er confents
    by ill Advice to walk;
  Nor ftands in Sinner's Way; nor fits
    where Men profanely talk!
2 But makes the perfect Law of God
    his Bufinefs and Delight;
  Devoutly reads therein by Day,
    and meditates by Night.
3 Like fome fair Tree, which, fed by Streams,
    with timely Fruit does bend;
  He ftill fhall flourifh, and Succefs
    all his Defigns attend.
4 Ungodly Men, and their Attempts,
    no lafting Root fhall find;
  Untimely blafted, and difpers'd
    like Chaff before the Wind.
5 Their Guilt fhall ftrike the Wicked dumb
    before their Judge's Face;
  No formal Hypocrite fhall then
    among the Saints have Place.
6 For God approves the juft Man's Ways;
    to Happinefs they tend;
  But Sinners, and the Paths they tread,
    fhall both in Ruin end.

PSALM II.

1 WITH reftlefs and ungovern'd Rage
    why do the Heathen ftorm?
  Why in fuch rafh Attempts engage,
    As they can ne'er perform?
2 The Great in Counfel, and in Might,
    their various Forces bring;
  Againft the Lord they all unite,
    and his anointed King.

PSALM ii.

3 " Muſt we ſubmit to their Commands?"
   preſumptuouſly they ſay:
  " No, let us break their ſlaviſh Bands,
  " and caſt their Chains away."

4 But God, who ſits enthron'd on high,
   and ſees how they combine,
  Does their conſpiring Strength defy,
   and mocks their vain Deſign.

5 Thick Clouds of Wrath divine ſhall break
   on his rebellious Foes;
  And thus will He in Thunder ſpeak
   to all that dare oppoſe:

6 " Tho' madly you diſpute my Will,
  " the King that I ordain,
  " Whoſe Throne is fix'd on *Sion's* Hill,
  " ſhall there ſecurely reign."

7 Attend, O Earth, whilſt I declare
   God's uncontroul'd Decree:
  " Thou art my Son; this Day my Heir
  " have I begotten thee.

8 " Aſk, and receive thy full Demands;
  " thine ſhall the Heathen be;
  " The utmoſt Limits of the Lands
  " ſhall be poſſeſs'd by thee.

9 " Thy threat'ning Sceptre thou ſhalt ſhake,
  " and cruſh them ev'ry where;
  " As maſſy Bars of Iron break
  " The Potter's brittle Ware."

10 Learn then, ye Princes, and give Ear,
   ye Judges of the Earth;

11 Worſhip the Lord with holy Fear;
   rejoice with awful Mirth.

12 Appeaſe the Son with due Reſpect,
   your timely Homage pay;
  Leſt he revenge the bold Neglect,
   incens'd by your Delay.

13 If but in Part his Anger riſe,
   Who can endure the Flame?
  Then bleſt are they, whoſe Hope relies
   on his moſt holy Name.

PSALM III.

1 HOW num'rous, Lord, of late are grown
    the Troublers of my Peace!
And as their Numbers hourly rife,
    fo does their Rage increafe.
2 Infulting, they my Soul upbraid,
    and Him whom I adore:
The God in whom he trufts, fay they,
    fhall refcue him no more.
3 But thou, O Lord, art my Defence;
    on Thee my Hopes rely:
Thou art my Glory, and fhalt yet
    lift up my Head on high.
4 Since whenfoe'er, in like Diftrefs,
    to God I made my Pray'r,
He heard me from his holy Hill,
    Why fhould I now defpair?
5 Guarded by Him, I laid me down
    my fweet Repofe to take;
For I thro' Him fecurely fleep,
    thro' Him in Safety wake.
6 No Force nor Fury of my Foes
    my Courage fhall confound,
Were they as many Hofts as Men,
    that have befet me round.
7 Arife, and fave me, O my God,
    who oft haft own'd my Caufe,
And fcatter'd oft thofe Foes to me
    and to thy righteous Laws.
8 Salvation to the Lord belongs:
    He only can defend:
His Bleffing he extends to all,
    that on his Pow'r depend.

PSALM IV.

1 O Lord, Thou art my righteous Judge,
    to my Complaint give Ear;
Thou ftill redeem'ft me from Diftrefs;
    have Mercy, Lord, and hear.

PSALM iv, v.

2 How long will ye, O Sons of Men,
  to blot my Fame devise?
  How long your vain Designs pursue,
  and spread malicious Lies?
3 Consider, that the righteous Man
  is God's peculiar Choice;
  And, when to him I make my Pray'r,
  He always hears my Voice.
4 Then stand in Awe of his Commands,
  flee ev'ry Thing that's ill;
  Commune in private with your Hearts,
  and bend them to his Will.
5 The Place of other Sacrifice
  let Righteousness supply;
  And let your Hope, securely fix'd,
  on God alone rely.
6 While worldly Minds impatient grow
  more prosp'rous Times to see;
  Still let the Glories of thy Face
  shine brightly, Lord, on me.
7 So shall my Heart o'erflow with Joy,
  more lasting and more true
  Than theirs, who Stores of Corn and Wine
  successively renew.
8 Then down in Peace I'll lay my Head,
  and take my needful Rest:
  No other Guard, O Lord, I crave,
  of thy Defence possess'd.

PSALM V.

1 LORD, hear the Voice of my Complaint,
   accept my secret Pray'r:
2 To Thee alone, my King, my God,
   will I for Help repair.
3 Thou in the Morn my Voice shalt hear,
   and with the dawning Day
   To Thee devoutly I'll look up,
   to Thee devoutly pray.
4 For Thou the Wrongs that I sustain
   canst never, Lord, approve,
   Who from thy sacred Dwelling-place
   all Evil dost remove.

5 Not long shall stubborn Fools remain
 unpunish'd in thy View;
 All such, as act unrighteous Things,
 thy Vengeance shall pursue.
6 The sland'ring Tongue, O God of Truth!
 by Thee shall be destroy'd;
 Who hat'st alike the Man in Blood
 and in Deceit employ'd.
7 But when thy boundless Grace shall me
 to thy lov'd Courts restore,
 On Thee I'll fix my longing Eyes,
 and humbly there adore.
8 Conduct me by thy righteous Laws;
 for watchful is my Foe:
 Therefore, O Lord, make plain the Way,
 wherein I ought to go.
9 Their Mouths vent nothing but Deceit,
 their Heart is set on Wrong:
 Their Throat is a devouring Grave,
 they flatter with their Tongue.
10 By their own Counsels let them fall,
 oppress'd with Loads of Sin;
 For they against thy righteous Laws
 have harden'd Rebels been.
11 But let all those, that trust in Thee,
 with Shouts their Joy proclaim;
 Let them rejoice, whom Thou preserv'st,
 and all that love thy Name.
12 To righteous Men the righteous Lord
 his Blessing will extend;
 And with his Favour all his Saints,
 as with a Shield, defend.

PSALM VI.

1 THY dreadful Anger, Lord, restrain,
 and spare a Wretch forlorn;
 Correct me not in thy fierce Wrath,
 too heavy to be borne.
2 Have Mercy, Lord, for I grow faint;
 unable to endure
 The Anguish of my aching Bones,
 which Thou alone canst cure.

PSALM vj, vij.

3 My tortur'd Flesh distracts my Mind,
    and fills my Soul with Grief:
  But, Lord, how long wilt Thou delay
    to grant me thy Relief?
4 Thy wonted Goodness, Lord, repeat,
    and ease my troubled Soul;
  Lord, for thy wondrous Mercies' sake,
    vouchsafe to make me whole.
5 For after Death no more can I
    Thy glorious Acts proclaim;
  No Pris'ners of the silent Grave
    can magnify thy Name.
6 Quite tir'd with Pain, with Groaning faint,
    no Hope of Ease I see;
  The Night that quiets common Griefs
    is spent in Tears by me.
7 My Beauty fades, my Sight grows dim,
    my Eyes with Weakness close;
  Old Age o'ertakes me, whilst I think
    on my insulting Foes.
8 Depart, ye Wicked; in my Wrongs
    ye shall no more rejoice;
  For God, I find, accepts my Tears,
    and listens to my Voice.
9, 10 He hears, and grants my humble Pray'r;
    and they, that wish my Fall,
  Shall blush and rage to see, that God
    protects me from them all.

PSALM VII.

1 O LORD, my God, since I have plac'd
    my Trust alone in Thee,
  From all my Persecutors' Rage
    do Thou deliver me.
2 To save me from my threat'ning Foe,
    Lord, interpose thy Pow'r:
  Lest, like a savage Lion, he
    my helpless Soul devour.
3, 4 If I am guilty, or did e'er
    against his Peace combine;
  Nay, if I have not spar'd his Life,
    who sought unjustly mine;

5 Let

PSALM vii.

5 Let then to persecuting Foes
   my Soul become a Prey;
Let them to Earth tread down my Life,
   in Dust my Honour lay.
6 Arise, and let thine Anger, Lord,
   in my Defence engage;
Exalt thyself above my Foes,
   and their insulting Rage.
Awake, awake, in my Behalf
   the Judgment to dispense,
Which Thou hast righteously ordain'd
   for injur'd Innocence.
7 So to thy Throne adoring Crowds
   shall still for Justice fly:
O! therefore, for their Sakes, resume
   thy Judgment Seat on high.
8 Impartial Judge of all the World,
   I trust my Cause to Thee;
According to my just Deserts,
   so let thy Sentence be.
9 Let wicked Arts and wicked Men
   together be o'erthrown;
But guard the Just, thou God, to whom
   the Hearts of both are known.
10, 11 God me protects; not only me,
   but all of upright Heart;
And daily lays up Wrath for those,
   who from his Laws depart.
12 If they persist, He whets his Sword,
   His Bow stands ready bent;
13 Ev'n now, with swift Destruction wing'd,
   His pointed Shafts are sent.
14 The Plots are fruitless, which my Foe
   unjustly did conceive:
15 The Pit, he digg'd for me, has prov'd
   his own untimely Grave.
16 On his own Head his Spite returns,
   whilst I from Harm am free:
On him the Violence is fall'n,
   which he design'd for me.
17 Therefore will I the righteous Ways
   of Providence proclaim;

I'll

PSALM vii, viii, ix.

I'll sing the Praise of God most High,
and celebrate his Name.

PSALM VIII.

1 O Thou, to whom all Creatures bow
within this earthly Frame,
Thro' all the World how great art Thou!
how glorious is thy Name!
In Heav'n thy wondrous Acts are sung,
Nor fully reckon'd there;

2 And yet thou mak'st the infant Tongue
thy boundless Praise declare.
Thro' Thee the Weak confound the Strong,
and crush their haughty Foes;
And so Thou quell'st the wicked Throng,
That Thee and Thine oppose.

3 When Heav'n, thy beauteous Work on high,
employs my wond'ring Sight;
The Moon, that nightly rules the Sky,
with Stars of feebler Light;

4 What's Man (say I) that, Lord, thou lov'st
to keep him in thy Mind?
Or what his Offspring, that Thou prov'st
to them so wondrous kind?

5 Him next in Power Thou didst create
to thy celestial Train;

6 Ordain'd with Dignity and State
o'er all thy Works to reign.

7 They jointly own his pow'rful Sway;
the Beasts that prey or graze;

8 The Bird that wings its airy Way;
the Fish that cuts the Seas.

9 O Thou, to whom all Creatures bow
within this earthly Frame,
Thro' all the World how great art Thou!
how glorious is thy Name!

PSALM IX.

1 To celebrate thy Praise, O Lord,
I will my Heart prepare;
To all the list'ning World thy Works,
thy wondrous Works, declare.

2 The Thought of them shall to my Soul
   exalted Pleasure bring;
 Whilst to thy Name, O Thou most High,
   triumphant Praise I sing.
3 Thou mad'st my haughty Foes to turn
   their Backs in shameful Flight;
 Struck with thy Presence, down they fell;
   they perish'd at thy Sight.
4 Against insulting Foes advanc'd,
   Thou didst my Cause maintain;
 My Right asserting from thy Throne,
   where Truth and Justice reign.
5 The Insolence of Heathen Pride
   Thou hast reduc'd to Shame:
 Their wicked Offspring quite destroy'd,
   and blotted out their Name.
6 Mistaking Foes, your haughty Threats
   are to a Period come:
 Our City stands, which you design'd
   to make our common Tomb.
7, 8 The Lord for ever lives, who has
   his righteous Throne prepar'd,
 Impartial Justice to dispense,
   to punish or reward.
9 God is a constant sure Defence
   against oppressing Rage;
 As Troubles rise, his needful Aids
   in our Behalf engage.
10 All those, who have his Goodness prov'd,
   will in his Truth confide;
 Whose Mercy ne'er forsook the Man,
   that on his Help rely'd.
11 Sing Praises therefore to the Lord,
   from *Sion* his Abode;
 Proclaim his Deeds, till all the World
   confess no other God.

PART II.

12 When He Inquiry makes for Blood,
   He'll call the Poor to Mind;
 The injur'd humble Man's Complaint
   Relief from Him shall find.

13 Take Pity on my Troubles, Lord,
    which spiteful Foes create,
  Thou, that hast rescu'd me so oft
    from Death's devouring Gate.
14 In *Sion* then I'll sing thy Praise
    to all that love thy Name;
  And with loud Shouts of grateful Joy
    thy saving Pow'r proclaim.
15 Deep in the Pit, they digg'd for me
    the Heathen Pride is laid;
  Their guilty Feet to their own Snare
    insensibly betray'd.
16 Thus, by the just Returns He makes,
    the mighty Lord is known;
  While wicked Men, by their own Plots,
    are shamefully o'erthrown.
17 No single Sinner shall escape,
    by Privacy obscur'd;
  No Nation, from his just Revenge,
    by Numbers be secur'd.
18 His suff'ring Saints, when most distress'd,
    He ne'er forgets to aid;
  Their Expectation shall be crown'd,
    tho' for a Time delay'd.
19 Arise, O Lord, assert thy Pow'r,
    and let not Man o'ercome;
  Descend to Judgment, and pronounce
    the guilty Heathen's Doom.
20 Strike Terror thro' the Nations round,
    till, by consenting Fear,
  They to each other, and themselves,
    but mortal Men appear.

PSALM X.

1 THY Presence why withdraw'st Thou,
      why hid'st Thou now thy Face, [Lord?
  When dismal Times of deep Distress
    call for thy wonted Grace?
2 The Wicked, swell'd with lawless Pride,
    have made the Poor their Prey:
  O let them fall by those Designs,
    which they for others lay:

3 For

PSALM x.

3 For strait they triumph, if Success
   their thriving Crimes attend:
And sordid Wretches, whom God hates,
   perversely they commend.
4 To own a Pow'r above themselves
   their haughty Pride disdains;
And therefore in their stubborn Mind
   no Thought of God remains.
5 Oppressive Methods they pursue,
   and all their Foes they slight;
Because thy Judgments unobserv'd
   are far above their Sight.
6 They fondly think, their prosp'rous State
   shall unmolested be;
They think, their vain Designs shall thrive,
   from all Misfortunes free.
7 Vain and deceitful is their Speech,
   with Curses fill'd, and Lies;
By which the Mischief of their Heart
   they study to disguise.
8 Near public Roads they lie conceal'd,
   and all their Art employ,
The Innocent and Poor at once
   to rifle and destroy.
9 Not Lions, couching in their Dens,
   surprize their heedless Prey
With greater Cunning, or express
   more savage Rage than they.
10 Sometimes they act the harmless Man,
   and modest Looks they wear;
That, so deceiv'd, the Poor may less
   their sudden Onset fear.

PART II.

11 For God, they think, no Notice takes
   of their unrighteous Deeds;
He never minds the suff'ring Poor,
   nor their Oppression heeds.
12 But Thou, O Lord, at length arise!
   stretch forth thy mighty Arm!
And, by the Greatness of thy Pow'r,
   defend the Poor from Harm.

13 No longer let the Wicked vaunt,
  and, proudly boasting, say,
  " Tush, God regards not what we do;
  " He never will repay."
14 Surely Thou seeſt, and all their Deeds
  impartially doſt try;
  The Orphan, therefore, and the Poor
  on Thee for Aid rely.
15 Defenceleſs let the Wicked fall,
  of all their Strength bereft;
  Confound, O God, their dark Deſigns,
  till no Remains are left.
16 Aſſert thy juſt Dominion, Lord,
  which ſhall for ever ſtand;
  Thou, who the Heathen didſt expel
  from this thy choſen Land.
17 Thou doſt the humble Suppliants hear,
  that to thy Throne repair;
  Thou firſt prepar'ſt their Hearts to pray,
  and then accept'ſt their Pray'r.
18 Thou in thy righteous Judgment weigh'ſt
  the Fatherleſs and Poor;
  That ſo the Tyrants of the Earth
  may perſecute no more.

PSALM XI.

1 SINCE I have plac'd my Truſt in God,
    a Refuge always nigh,
  Why ſhould I, like a tim'rous Bird,
    to diſtant Mountains fly?
2 Behold, the Wicked bend their Bow,
    and ready fix their Dart;
  Lurking in Ambuſh to deſtroy
    the Man of upright Heart.
3 When once the firm Aſſurance fails,
    which Public Faith imparts,
  'Tis Time for Innocence to fly
    from ſuch deceitful Arts.
4 The Lord hath both a Temple here,
    and righteous Throne above;
  Where he ſurveys the Sons of Men,
    and how their Counſels move.

5 If God the Righteous, whom He loves,
  for Trial does correct,
  What must the Sons of Violence,
  whom He abhors, expect?
6 Snares, Fire, and Brimstone, on their Heads
  shall in one Tempest show'r;
  This dreadful Mixture his Revenge
  into their Cup shall pour.
7 The righteous Lord will righteous Deeds
  with signal Favour grace;
  And to the upright Man disclose
  the Brightness of his Face.

PSALM XII.

1 SINCE godly Men decay, O Lord,
    do Thou my Cause defend;
  For scarce these wretched Times afford
    one just and faithful Friend.
2 One Neighbour, now, can scarce believe
    what t'other does impart:
  With flatt'ring Lips they all deceive,
    and with a double Heart.
3 But Lips, that with Deceit abound,
    can never prosper long;
  God's righteous Vengeance will confound
    the proud blaspheming Tongue.
4 In vain those foolish Boasters say,
    " Our Tongues are sure our own;
  " With doubtful Words we'll still betray,
  " and be controul'd by none."
5 For God, who hears the suff'ring Poor,
    and their Oppression knows,
  Will soon arise, and give them Rest,
    in Spite of all their Foes.
6 The Word of God shall still abide,
    and void of Falshood be;
  As is the Silver, sev'n Times try'd,
    from drossy Mixture free.
7 The Promise of his aiding Grace
    shall reach its purpos'd End:
  His Servants from this faithless Race
    He ever shall defend.

8 Then

8 Then shall the Wicked be perplex'd,
  nor know which Way to fly;
When those, whom they despis'd and vex'd,
  shall be advanc'd on high.

PSALM XIII.

1 HOW long wilt Thou forget me, Lord?
    must I for ever mourn?
How long wilt Thou withdraw from me,
  oh, never to return?
2 How long shall anxious Thoughts my Soul,
  and Grief my Heart, oppress?
How long my Enemies insult,
  and I have no Redress?
3 Oh, hear! and to my longing Eyes
  restore thy wonted Light;
And suddenly, or I shall sleep
  in everlasting Night.
4 Restore me, lest they proudly boast
  'twas their own Strength o'ercame:
Permit not them, that vex my Soul,
  to triumph in my Shame.
5 Since I have always plac'd my Trust
  beneath thy Mercy's Wing;
Thy saving Health will come; and then
  my Heart with Joy shall spring.
6 Then shall my Song, with Praise inspir'd,
  to Thee my God ascend;
Who to thy Servant in Distress
  such Bounty didst extend.

PSALM XIV.

1 SURE, wicked Fools must needs suppose,
    that God is nothing but a Name:
Corrupt and lewd their Practice grows;
  no Breast is warm'd with holy Flame.
2 The Lord look'd down from Heav'n's high
  and all the Sons of Men did view, [Tow'r,
To see if any own'd his Pow'r,
  if any Truth or Justice knew.
3 But all, he saw, were gone aside,
  all were degen'rate grown and base:

None

PSALM xiv, xv.

None took Religion for their Guide,
   not one of all the sinful Race.
4 But can these Workers of Deceit
   be all so dull and senseless grown,
That they, like Bread, my People eat,
   and God's Almighty Pow'r disown?
5 How will they tremble then for Fear,
   when his just Wrath shall them o'ertake?
For, to the Righteous God is near,
   and never will their Cause forsake.
6 Ill Men, in vain, with Scorn expose
   those Methods, which the Good pursue,
Since God a Refuge is for those
   whom his just Eyes with Favour view.
7 Would He his saving Pow'r employ
   to break his People's servile Band;
Then Shouts of universal Joy
   Should loudly echo thro' the Land.

PSALM XV.

1 LORD, who's the happy Man, that may
      to thy bless'd Courts repair;
Not, Stranger like, to visit them,
   but to inhabit there?
2 'Tis he, whose ev'ry Thought and Deed
   by Rules of Virtue moves;
Whose gen'rous Tongue disdains to speak
   the Thing his Heart disproves.
3 Who never did a Slander forge
   his Neighbour's Fame to wound;
Or hearken to a false Report,
   by Malice whisper'd round.
4 Who Vice, in all its Pomp and Pow'r,
   can treat with just Neglect;
And Piety, tho' cloth'd in Rags,
   religiously respect.
5 Who to his plighted Vows and Trust
   has ever firmly stood;
And tho' he promise to his Loss,
   He makes his Promise good.
6 Whose Soul in Usury disdains
   his Treasure to employ;

B   Whom

* Whom no Rewards can ever bribe
 the Guiltless to destroy.
7 The Man, who by his steady Course
 has Happiness ensur'd,
 When Earth's Foundation shakes, shall stand
 by Providence secur'd.

PSALM XVI.

1 PROTECT me from my cruel Foes,
 and shield me, Lord, from Harm;
 Because my Trust I still repose
 on thy Almighty Arm.
2 My Soul all Help but thine does slight,
 all Gods but Thee disown;
 Yet can no Deeds of mine requite
 the Goodness Thou hast shown.
3 But those that strictly virtuous are,
 and love the Thing that's right,
 To favour always, and prefer,
 shall be my chief Delight.
4 How shall their Sorrows be increas'd
 who other Gods adore!
 Their bloody Off'rings I detest,
 their very Name abhor.
5 My Lot is fall'n in that blest Land,
 where God is truly known;
 He fills my Cup with lib'ral Hand:
 'tis He supports my Throne.
6 In Nature's most delightful Scene
 my happy Portion lies:
 The Place of my appointed Reign
 all other Lands outvies.
7 Therefore my Soul shall bless the Lord,
 whose Precepts give me Light;
 And private Counsel still afford,
 in Sorrow's dismal Night.
8 I strive each Action to approve
 to his all-seeing Eye:
 No Danger shall my Hopes remove,
 because He still is nigh.
9 Therefore my Heart all Grief defies,
 my Glory does rejoice:

My

My Flesh shall rest, in Hope to rise,
    wak'd by his pow'rful Voice.
10 Thou, Lord, when I resign my Breath,
    my Soul from Hell shalt free;
Nor let thy Holy One in Death
    the least Corruption see.
11 Thou shalt the Paths of Life display,
    that to thy Presence lead;
Where Pleasures dwell without Allay,
    and Joys that never fade.

PSALM XVII.

1 TO my just Plea and sad Complaint
    attend, O righteous Lord;
And to my Pray'r, as 'tis unfeign'd,
    a gracious Ear afford.
2 As in thy Sight I am approv'd,
    so let my Sentence be;
And with impartial Eyes, O Lord,
    my upright Dealing see.
3 For Thou hast search'd my Heart by Day,
    and visited by Night;
And on the strictest Trial found
    its secret Motions right.
Nor shall thy Justice, Lord, alone
    my Heart's Designs acquit;
For I have purpos'd that my Tongue
    shall no Offence commit.
4 I know what wicked Men would do,
    their Safety to maintain;
But me thy just and mild Commands
    from bloody Paths restrain.
5 That I may still, in Spite of Wrongs,
    my Innocence secure,
O guide me in thy righteous Ways,
    and make my Footsteps sure.
6 Since, heretofore, I ne'er in vain
    to Thee my Pray'r addres'd;
O! now, my God, incline thine Ear
    to this my just Request.
7 The Wonders of thy Truth and Love
    in my Defence engage;

PSALM xvii, xviii.

Thou whose Right-hand preserves thy Saints
from their Oppressors' Rage.

PART II.

8, 9 O! keep me in thy tend'rest Care;
 thy shelt'ring Wings stretch out,
To guard me safe from savage Foes,
 that compass me about.
10 O'ergrown with Luxury, inclos'd
 in their own Fat they lie;
And with a proud blaspheming Mouth
 both God and Man defy.
11 Well may they boast; for they have now
 my Paths encompass'd round;
Their Eyes at watch, their Bodies bow'd,
 and couching on the Ground.
12 In posture of a Lion set,
 when greedy of his Prey;
Or a young Lion, when he lurks
 within a covert Way.
13 Arise, O Lord, defeat their Plots,
 their swelling Rage control:
From wicked Men, who are thy Sword,
 deliver Thou my Soul.
14 From worldly Men, thy sharpest Scourge,
 whose Portion's here below:
Who, fill'd with earthly Stores, aspire
 no other Bliss to know.
15 Their Race is num'rous, that partake
 their Substance while they live;
Their Heirs survive, to whom they may
 the vast Remainder give.
16 But I, in Uprightness, thy Face
 shall view without Control;
And waking, shall its Image find
 reflected in my Soul.

PSALM XVIII.

1, 2 NO Change of Times shall ever shock
  my firm Affection, Lord, to Thee;
For Thou hast always been a Rock,
 a Fortress and Defence to me.

PSALM xviii.

Thou my Deliv'rer art, my God;
   my Truſt is in thy mighty Pow'r:
Thou art my Shield from Foes abroad,
   at Home my Safeguard and my Tow'r.
3 To Thee I will addreſs my Pray'r,
   (to whom all Praiſe we juſtly owe;)
So ſhall I, by thy watchful Care,
   be guarded from my treach'rous Foe.
4, 5 By Floods of wicked Men diſtreſs'd,
   with deadly Sorrows compaſs'd round,
With dire infernal Pangs oppreſs'd,
   in Death's unwieldy Fetters bound;
6 To Heav'n I made my mournful Pray'r,
   to God addreſs'd my humble Moan;
Who gracioufly inclin'd his Ear,
   and heard me from his lofty Throne.

PART II.

7 When God aroſe to take my Part,
   the conſcious Earth did quake with Fear;
From their firm Poſts the Hills did ſtart,
   nor could his dreadful Fury bear.
8 Thick Clouds of Smoke difpers'd abroad,
   Enſigns of Wrath before him came;
Devouring Fire around him glow'd,
   that Coals were kindled at the Flame.
9 He left the beauteous Realms of Light,
   whilſt Heav'n bow'd down its awful Head;
Beneath his Feet ſubſtantial Night
   was like a ſable Carpet ſpread.
10 The Chariot of the KING of Kings,
   which active Troops of Angels drew,
On a ſtrong Tempeſt's rapid Wings
   with moſt amazing Swiftneſs flew.
11, 12 Black wat'ry Miſts and Clouds conſpir'd
   with thickeſt Shades his Face to veil;
But at his Brightneſs ſoon retir'd,
   and fell in Show'rs of Fire and Hail.
13 Thro' Heav'n's wide Arch a thund'ring Peal,
   God's angry Voice did loudly roar;
While Earth's ſad Face with Heaps of Hail,
   and Flakes of Fire, was cover'd o'er.

14 His ſharpen'd Arrows round He threw,
   which made his ſcatter'd Foes retreat;
Like Darts his nimble Lightning flew,
   and quickly finiſh'd their Defeat.
15 The Deep its ſecret Stores diſclos'd;
   The World's Foundations naked lay,
By his avenging Wrath expos'd;
   which fiercely rag'd that dreadful Day.

PART III.

16 The Lord did on my Side engage;
   from Heav'n, his Throne, my Cauſe upheld;
And ſnatch'd me from the furious Rage
   of threat'ning Waves, that proudly ſwell'd.
17 God his reſiſtleſs Pow'r employ'd
   my ſtrongeſt Foes Attempts to break;
Who elſe with Eaſe had ſoon deſtroy'd
   The weak Defence that I could make.
18 Their ſubtle Rage had near prevail'd,
   when I diſtreſs'd and friendleſs lay;
But ſtill, when other Succours fail'd,
   God was my firm Support and Stay.
19 From Dangers that incloſ'd me round,
   He brought me forth, and ſet me free;
For ſome juſt Cauſe his Goodneſs found,
   That mov'd him to delight in me.
20 Becauſe in me no Guilt remains,
   God does his gracious Help extend:
My Hands are free from bloody Stains;
   therefore the Lord is ſtill my Friend.
21, 22 For I his Judgments kept in Sight,
   in his juſt Paths I always trod;
I never did his Statutes ſlight,
   nor looſely wander'd from my God.
23, 24 But ſtill my Soul, ſincere and pure,
   did ev'n from darling Sins refrain:
His Favours therefore yet endure,
   becauſe my Heart and Hands are clean.

PART IV.

25, 26 Thou ſuit'ſt, O Lord, thy righteous Ways
   to virtuous Paths of Human-kind:

They

They, who for Mercy merit Praife,
   with Thee fhall wondrous Mercy find.
Thou to the Juft fhalt Juftice fhow,
   the Pure thy Purity fhall fee;
Such as perverfely chufe to go,
   fhall meet with due Returns from Thee.

27, 28 That He the humble Soul will fave,
   and crufh the Haughty's boafted Might,
In me the Lord an Inftance gave,
   whofe Darknefs he has turn'd to Light.

29 On his firm Succour I rely'd,
   and did o'er num'rous Foes prevail;
Nor fear'd, whilft He was on my Side,
   the beft-defended Walls to fcale.

30 For God's Defigns fhall ftill fucceed;
   his Word will bear the utmoft Teft;
He's a ftrong Shield to all that need,
   and on his fure Protection reft.

31 Who then deferves to be ador'd,
   But God, on whom my Hopes depend?
Or who, except the mighty Lord,
   can with refiftlefs Pow'r defend?

PART V.

32, 33 'Tis God that girds my Armour on,
   and all my juft Defigns fulfils:
Thro' Him my Feet can fwiftly run,
   and nimbly climb the fteepeft Hills.

34 Leffons of War from Him I take,
   and manly Weapons learn to wield;
Strong Bows of Steel with Eafe I break,
   forc'd by my ftronger Arms to yield.

35 The Buckler of his faving Health
   protects me from affaulting Foes:
His Hand fuftains me ftill; my Wealth
   and Greatnefs from his Bounty flows.

36 My Goings He enlarg'd abroad,
   till then to narrow Paths confin'd;
And, when in flipp'ry Ways I trod,
   the Method of my Steps defign'd.

37 Thro' Him I num'rous Hofts defeat,
   and flying Squadrons captive take;

PSALM xviii.

Nor from my fierce Purſuit retreat,
 till I a final Conqueſt make.
38 Cover'd with Wounds, in vain they try
 their vanquiſh'd Heads again to rear:
Spite of their boaſted Strength, they lie
 beneath my Feet, and grovel there.
39 God, when freſh Armies take the Field,
 recruits my Strength, my Courage warms;
He makes my ſtrong Oppoſers yield,
 ſubdu'd by my prevailing Arms.
40 Thro' Him the Necks of proſtrate Foes
 my conqu'ring Feet in Triumph preſs:
Aided by him, I root out thoſe
 who hate and envy my Succeſs.
41 With loud Complaints all Friends they try'd;
 but none was able to defend:
At length to God for Help they cry'd;
 but God would no Aſſiſtance lend.
42 Like flying Duſt, which Winds purſue,
 their broken Troops I ſcatter'd round:
Their ſlaughter'd Bodies forth I threw,
 like loathſome Dirt that clogs the Ground.

PART VI.

43 Our factious Tribes, at Strife till now,
 by God's Appointment me obey:
The Heathen to my Sceptre bow,
 and Foreign Nations own my Sway.
44 Remoteſt Realms their Homage ſend,
 when my ſucceſsful Name they hear;
Strangers for my Commands attend,
 charm'd with Reſpect, or aw'd by Fear.
45 All to my Summons timely yield,
 or ſoon in Battle are diſmay'd;
For ſtronger Holds they quit the Field,
 and ſtill in ſtrongeſt Holds afraid.
46 Let the Eternal Lord be prais'd,
 the Rock, on whoſe Defence I reſt!
O'er higheſt Heav'n his Name be rais'd,
 who me with his Salvation bleſs'd!
47 'Tis God that ſtill ſupports my Right;
 his juſt Revenge my Foes purſues;

'Tis

PSALM xix.

'Tis He that, with resistless Might,
    fierce Nations to my Yoke subdues.
48 My universal Safeguard He!
    From whom my lasting Honours flow;
He made me great, and set me free
    from my remorseless bloody Foe.
49 Therefore, to celebrate his Fame
    my grateful Voice to Heav'n I'll raise:
And Nations, Strangers to his Name,
    shall thus be taught to sing his Praise.
50 " God to his King Deliv'rance sends;
    " shews his Anointed signal Grace:
" His Mercy evermore extends
    " to *David* and his promis'd Race."

PSALM XIX.

1 THE Heav'ns declare thy Glory, Lord,
    which that alone can fill;
The Firmament and Stars express
    their great Creator's Skill.
2 The Dawn of each returning Day
    fresh Beams of Knowledge brings;
From darkest Night's successive Rounds
    divine Instruction springs.
3 Their pow'rful Language to no Realm
    or Region is confin'd;
'Tis Nature's Voice, and understood
    alike by all Mankind.
4 Their Doctrine does its sacred Sense
    thro' Earth's Extent display;
Whose bright Contents the circling Sun
    does round the World convey.
5 No Bridegroom, for his Nuptials dress'd,
    has such a cheerful Face:
No Giant doth like him rejoice
    to run his glorious Race.
6 From East to West, from West to East,
    his restless Course he goes;
And, thro' his Progress, cheerful Light
    and vital Warmth bestows.

PART

PART II.

7 God's perfect Law converts the Soul,
  reclaims from false Desires;
  With sacred Wisdom his sure Word
  the Ignorant inspires.
8 The Statutes of the Lord are just,
  and bring sincere Delight:
  His pure Commands in Search of Truth
  assist the feeblest Sight.
9 His perfect Worship here is fix'd,
  on sure Foundations laid:
  His equal Laws are in the Scales
  of Truth and Justice weigh'd.
10 Of more Esteem than golden Mines,
  or Gold refin'd with Skill;
  More sweet than Honey, or the Drops
  that from the Comb distil.
11 My trusty Counsellors they are,
  and friendly Warnings give;
  Divine Rewards attend on those
  who by thy Precepts live.
12 But what frail Man observes how oft
  he does from Virtue fall?
  O! cleanse me from my secret Faults,
  thou God that know'st them all.
13 Let no presumptuous Sin, O Lord,
  Dominion have o'er me;
  That, by thy Grace preserv'd, I may
  the great Transgression flee.
14 So shall my Pray'r and Praises be
  with thy Acceptance blest;
  And I, secure on thy Defence,
  my Strength and Saviour, rest.

PSALM XX.

1 THE Lord to thy Request attend,
  and hear thee in Distress:
  The Name of *Jacob's* God defend,
  and grant thy Arms Success.
2 To aid thee from on High repair,
  and Strength from *Sion* give;

3 Remember

PSALM xx, xxi.

3 Remember all thy Off'rings there,
   thy Sacrifice receive.
4 To compass thy own Heart's Desire
   thy Counsels still direct;
   May kindly all Events conspire
   to bring them to Effect.
5 To thy Salvation, Lord, for Aid
   we chearfully repair,
   With Banners in thy Name display'd,
   " the Lord accept thy Pray'r."
6 Our Hopes are fix'd, that now the Lord
   our Sov'reign will defend;
   From Heav'n resistless Aid afford,
   and to his Pray'r attend.
7 Some trust in Steeds for War design'd;
   on Chariots some rely:
   Against them all we'll call to mind
   the Pow'r of God most high.
8 But from their Steeds and Chariots thrown,
   behold them thro' the Plain,
   Disorder'd, broke, and trampled down,
   whilst firm our Troops remain.
9 Still save us, Lord, and still proceed
   our rightful Cause to bless:
   Hear, King of Heav'n, in Times of Need,
   the Pray'r that we address.

PSALM XXI.

1 THE King, O Lord, with Songs of Praise
      shall in thy Strength rejoice;
   With thy Salvation crown'd, shall raise
      to Heav'n his cheerful Voice.
2 For Thou, whate'er his Lips request,
      not only dost impart;
   But hast with thy Acceptance blest
      the Wishes of his Heart.
3 Thy Goodness and thy tender Care
      have all his Hopes outgone;
   A Crown of Gold Thou mad'st him wear,
      and fett'dst it firmly on.
4 He pray'd for Life; and Thou, O Lord,
      didst to his Prayer attend,

And

PSALM xxi.

    And graciously to him afford
      a Life that ne'er shall end.
5 Thy sure Defence through Nations round
      has spread his glorious Name;
    And his successful Actions crown'd
      with Majesty and Fame.
6 Eternal Blessings Thou bestow'st,
      and mak'st his Joys increase;
    Whilst Thou to him unclouded show'st
      the Brightness of thy Face.

PART II.

7 Because the King on God alone
      for timely Aid relies;
    His Mercy still supports his Throne,
      and all his Wants supplies.
8 But, righteous Lord, thy stubborn Foes
      shall feel thy heavy Hand;
    Thy vengeful Arm shall find out those
      that hate thy mild Command.
9 When Thou against them dost engage,
      thy just, but dreadful Doom
    Shall, like a glowing Oven's Rage,
      their Hopes and them consume.
10 Nor shall thy furious Anger cease,
      or with their Ruin end;
    But root out all their guilty Race,
      and to their Seed extend.
11 For all their Thoughts were set on Ill,
      their Hearts on Malice bent,
    But Thou with watchful Care didst still
      the ill Effects prevent.
12 In vain by shameful Flight they'll try
      to 'scape thy dreadful Might,
    While thy swift Darts shall faster fly,
      and gall them in their Flight.
13 Thus, Lord, thy wondrous Strength disclose,
      and thus exalt thy Fame;
    Whilst we glad Songs of Praise compose
      to thy Almighty Name.

PSALM XXII.

1 MY God, my God, why leav'ſt Thou me,
  when I with Anguiſh faint?
  O! why ſo far from me remov'd,
  and from my loud Complaint?
2 All Day, but all the Day unheard,
  To Thee do I complain;
  With Cries implore Relief all Night,
  but cry all Night in vain.
3 Yet Thou art ſtill the righteous Judge
  of Innocence oppreſs'd:
  And therefore *Iſrael's* Praiſes are
  of Right to Thee addreſs'd.
4, 5 On Thee our Anceſtors rely'd,
  and thy Deliv'rance found;
  With pious Confidence they pray'd,
  and with Succeſs were crown'd.
6 But I am treated like a Worm;
  like none of human Birth:
  Not only by the Great revil'd,
  but made the Rabble's Mirth.
7 With Laughter all the gazing Crowd
  my Agonies ſurvey;
  They ſhoot the Lip, they ſhake the Head,
  and thus deriding ſay:
8 " In God he truſted, boaſting oft,
  " that he was Heav'n's Delight;
  " Let God come down to ſave him now,
  " and own his Favourite."

PART II.

9 Thou mad'ſt my teeming Mother's Womb
  a living Offspring bear;
  When but a Suckling at the Breaſt
  I was thy early Care.
10 Thou, Guardian-like, didſt ſhield from Wrongs
  my helpleſs infant Days;
  And ſince haſt been my God, and Guide
  thro' Life's bewilder'd Ways.
11 Withdraw not then ſo far from me,
  when Trouble is ſo nigh:

O ſend

PSALM xxii.

O send me Help! thy Help, on which
    I only can rely.
12 High-pamper'd Bulls, a frowning Herd,
    from *Basan's* Forest met,
With Strength proportion'd to their Rage,
    have me around beset.
13 They gape on me, and every Mouth
    a yawning Grave appears;
The Desart Lion's savage Roar
    less dreadful is than theirs.

PART III.

14 My Blood like Water's spill'd, my Joints
    are rack'd and out of Frame;
My Heart dissolves within my Breast,
    like Wax before the Flame.
15 My Strength like Potter's Earth is parch'd,
    my Tongue cleaves to my Jaws;
And to the silent Shades of Death
    my fainting Soul withdraws.
16 Like Blood-hounds, to surround me, they
    in pack'd Assemblies meet;
They pierc'd my inoffensive Hands,
    they pierc'd my harmless Feet.
17 My Body's rack'd, till all my Bones
    distinctly may be told:
Yet such a Spectacle of Woe
    as Pastime they behold.
18 As Spoil my Garments they divide,
    Lots for my Vesture cast:
19 Therefore approach, O Lord, my Strength,
    and to my Succour haste.
20 From their sharp Swords protect Thou me:
    (of all but Life bereft!)
Nor let my Darling in the Pow'r
    of cruel Dogs be left.
21 To save me from the Lion's Jaws
    thy present Succour send:
As once from goring Unicorns
    Thou didst my Life defend.
22 Then to my Brethren I'll declare
    the Triumph of thy Name;

PSALM xxii.

In Presence of assembled Saints
   thy Glory thus proclaim:
23 "Ye Worshipers of *Jacob's* God,
   " all you of *Israel's* Line,
   " O praise the Lord, and to your Praise
   " sincere Obedience join.
24 " He ne'er disdain'd on low Distress
   " to cast a gracious Eye;
   " Nor turn'd from Poverty his Face,
   " but heard its humble Cry."

PART IV.

25 Thus in thy sacred Courts will I
   my cheerful Thanks express;
   In Presence of thy Saints perform
   the Vows of my Distress.
26 The meek Companions of my Grief
   shall find my Table spread;
   And all that seek the Lord shall be
   with Joys immortal fed.
27 Then shall the glad converted World
   to God their Homage pay;
   And scatter'd Nations of the Earth
   one Sovereign Lord obey.
28 'Tis his supreme Prerogative
   o'er Subject Kings to reign:
   'Tis just that He should rule the World,
   who does the World sustain.
29 The Rich who are with Plenty fed,
   his Bounty must confess;
   The Sons of Want, by him reliev'd,
   their gen'rous Patron bless.
   With humble Worship to his Throne
   they all for Aid resort:
   That Pow'r, which first their Beings gave,
   can only them support.
30, 31 Then shall a chosen spotless Race,
   devoted to his Name,
   To their admiring Heirs, his Truth
   and glorious Acts proclaim.

PSALM XXIII.

1 THE Lord Himself, the mighty Lord,
    vouchsafes to be my Guide;
The Shepherd, by whose constant Care
    my Wants are all supply'd.
2 In tender Grass He makes me feed,
    and gently there repose;
Then leads me to cool Shades, and where
    refreshing Water flows,
3 He does my wand'ring Soul reclaim,
    and, to his endless Praise,
Instruct with humble Zeal to walk
    in his most righteous Ways.
4 I pass the gloomy Vale of Death,
    from Fear and Danger free;
For there his aiding Rod and Staff
    defend and comfort me.
5 In Presence of my spiteful Foes
    He does my Table spread:
He crowns my Cup with cheerful Wine,
    with Oil anoints my Head.
6 Since God doth thus his wondrous Love
    through all my Life extend,
That Life to Him I will devote,
    and in his Temple spend.

PSALM XXIV.

1 THIS spacious Earth is all the Lord's,
    the Lord her Fulness is.:
The World, and they that dwell therein,
    by Sov'reign Right are his.
2 He fram'd and fix'd it on the Seas,
    and his Almighty Hand
Upon inconstant Floods has made
    the stable Fabrick stand.
3 But for Himself this Lord of All
    one chosen Seat design'd:
O! who shall to thy sacred Hill
    desir'd Admittance find?
4. The Man whose Hands and Heart are pure,
    whose Thoughts from Pride are free;

PSALM xxiv, xxv.

Who honest Poverty prefers
   to gainful Perjury.
5 This, this is he, on whom the Lord
   shall show'r his Blessings down;
  Whom God his Saviour shall vouchsafe
   with Righteousness to crown.
6 Such is the Race of Saints, by whom
   the sacred Courts are trod;
  And such the Proselytes that seek
   the Face of *Jacob's* God.
7 Erect your Heads, Eternal Gates;
   unfold, to entertain
  The King of Glory: See! He comes
   with his Celestial Train.
8 Who is the King of Glory? Who?
   the Lord for Strength renown'd;
  In Battle mighty; o'er his Foes
   Eternal Victor crown'd.
9 Erect your Heads, ye Gates; unfold,
   in State to entertain
  The King of Glory: See! He comes
   with all his shining Train.
10 Who is the King of Glory? Who?
   the Lord of Hosts renown'd:
  Of Glory He alone is King,
   who is with Glory crown'd.

PSALM XXV.

1,2 TO God, in whom I trust,
   I lift my Heart and Voice;
  O! let me not be put to Shame,
   nor let my Foes rejoice.
3 Those who on Thee rely,
   let no Disgrace attend:
  Be that the shameful Lot of such
   as wilfully offend.
4,5 To me thy Truth impart,
   and lead me in thy Way:
  For thou art He that brings me Help;
   on Thee I wait all Day.
6 Thy Mercies and thy Love,
   O Lord, recal to Mind:

PSALM xxv.

 And graciously continue still,
  as Thou wert ever, kind.
7 Let all my youthful Crimes
  be blotted out by Thee;
 And, for thy wondrous Goodness Sake,
  in Mercy think on me.
8 His Mercy, and his Truth,
  the righteous Lord displays,
 In bringing wand'ring Sinners Home,
  and teaching them his Ways.
9 He those in Justice guides,
  who his Direction seek;
 And in his sacred Paths shall lead
  the Humble and the Meek.
10 Thro' all the Ways of God
  both Truth and Mercy shine,
 To such as with religious Hearts
  to his bless'd Will incline.

PART II.

11 Since Mercy is the Grace
  that most exalts thy Fame,
 Forgive my heinous Sin, O Lord,
  and so advance thy Name.
12 Whoe'er with humble Fear
  to God his Duty pays,
 Shall find the Lord a faithful Guide
  in all his righteous Ways.
13 His quiet Soul with Peace
  shall be for ever bless'd;
 And by his num'rous Race the Land
  successively possess'd.
14 For God to all his Saints
  his secret Will imparts;
 And does his gracious Cov'nant write
  in their obedient Hearts.
15 To Him I lift my Eyes,
  and wait his timely Aid,
 Who breaks the strong and treach'rous Snare
  which for my Feet was laid.
16 O! turn, and all my Griefs,
  in Mercy, Lord, redress;

PSALM xxv, xxvi.

For I am compass'd round with Woes,
    and plung'd in deep Distress.
17 The Sorrows of my Heart
    to mighty Sums increase;
O! from this dark and dismal State
    my troubled Soul release!
18 Do Thou with tender Eyes
    my sad Affliction see;
Acquit me, Lord, and from my Guilt
    entirely set me free.
19 Consider, Lord, my Foes,
    how vast their Numbers grow!
What lawless Force and Rage they use,
    what boundless Hate they show.
20 Protect, and set my Soul
    from their fierce Malice free;
Nor let me be asham'd, who place
    my stedfast Trust in Thee.
21 Let all my righteous Acts
    to full Perfection rise;
Because my firm and constant Hope
    on Thee alone relies.
22 To *Israel's* chosen Race
    continue ever kind;
And in the Midst of all their Wants
    let them thy Succour find.

PSALM XXVI.

1 JUDGE me, O Lord, for I the Paths
    of Righteousness have trod;
I cannot fail, who all my Trust
    repose on Thee, my God.
2,3 Search, prove my Heart, whose Innocence
    will shine the more 'tis try'd:
For I have kept thy Grace in View,
    and made thy Truth my Guide.
4 I never for Companions took
    the Idle or Profane;
No Hypocrite, with all his Arts,
    could e'er my Friendship gain.
5 I hate the busy plotting Crew,
    who make distracted Times;

  And shun their wicked Company,
   as I avoid their Crimes.
6 I'll wash my Hands in Innocence,
  and bring an Heart so pure,
 That, when thy Altar I approach,
  my Welcome shall secure.
7, 8 My Thanks I'll publish there, and tell
  how thy Renown excels:
 That Seat affords me most Delight,
  in which thy Honour dwells.
9 Pass not on me the Sinners' Doom,
  who Murder make their Trade;
10 Who others' Rights, by secret Bribes
  or open Force, invade.
11 But I will walk in Paths of Truth,
  and Innocence pursue:
 Protect me, therefore, and to me
  thy Mercies, Lord, renew.
12 In spite of all assaulting Foes,
  I still maintain my Ground:
 And shall survive among thy Saints,
  thy Praises to resound.

PSALM XXVII.

1 WHOM should I fear, since God to me
  is saving Health and Light?
 Since strongly He my Life supports,
  what can my Soul affright?
2 With fierce Intent my Flesh to tear,
  when Foes beset me round,
 They stumbled, and their lofty Crests
  were made to strike the Ground;
3 Thro' Him my Heart undaunted dares
  with num'rous Hosts to cope;
 Thro' Him in doubtful Streights of War
  for good Success I hope.
4 Henceforth within his House to dwell
  I earnestly desire;
 His wondrous Beauty there to view,
  and his bless'd Will inquire.
5 For there may I with Comfort rest,
  in Times of deep Distress;

PSALM xxvii.

And safe as on a Rock abide
   in that secure Recess:
6 Whilst God o'er all my haughty Foes
   my lofty Head shall raise;
And I my joyful Tribute bring,
   with grateful Songs of Praise.

PART II.

7 Continue, Lord, to hear my Voice,
   whene'er to thee I cry;
In Mercy my Complaints receive,
   nor my Request deny.
8 When us to seek thy glorious Face
   Thou kindly dost advise;
" Thy glorious Face I'll always seek,"
   my grateful Heart replies.
9 Then hide not Thou thy Face, O Lord,
   nor me in Wrath reject;
My God and Saviour, leave not him
   Thou didst so oft protect.
10 Tho' all my Friends and nearest Kin
   their helpless Charge forsake;
Yet Thou, whose Love excels them all,
   wilt Care and Pity take.
11 Instruct me in thy Paths, O Lord;
   my Ways directly guide;
Lest envious Men, who watch my Steps,
   should see me tread aside.
12 Lord, disappoint my cruel Foes;
   defeat their ill Desire,
Whose lying Lips, and bloody Hands,
   against my Peace conspire.
13 I trusted that my future Life
   should with thy Love be crown'd;
Or else my fainting Soul had sunk,
   with Sorrow compass'd round.
14 God's Time with patient Faith expect,
   and He'll inspire thy Breast
With inward Strength: Do thou thy Part,
   and leave to Him the Rest.

PSALM XXVIII.

1 O LORD, my Rock, to Thee I cry,
   in Sighs confume my Breath:
O! anfwer, or I fhall become
   like thofe that fleep in Death.

2 Regard my Supplication, Lord,
   the Cries that I repeat,
With weeping Eyes, and lifted Hands,
   before thy Mercy-feat.

3 Let me efcape the Sinner's Doom,
   who make a Trade of Ill;
And ever fpeak the Perfon fair,
   whofe Blood they mean to fpill.

4 According to their Crime's Extent,
   let Juftice have its Courfe;
Relentlefs be to them, as they
   have finn'd without Remorfe.

5 Since they the Works of God defpife,
   nor will his Grace adore,
His Wrath fhall utterly deftroy,
   and build them up no more.

6 But I, with due Acknowledgment,
   his Praifes will refound;
From whom the Cries of my Diftrefs
   a gracious Anfwer found.

7 My Heart its Confidence repos'd
   in God, my Strength and Shield;
In Him I trufted, and return'd
   triumphant from the Field.
As He hath made my Joys complete,
   'tis juft that I fhould raife
The cheerful Tribute of my Thanks,
   and thus refound his Praife:

8 " His aiding Pow'r fupport the Troops
   " that my juft Caufe maintain:
" 'Twas He advanc'd me to the Throne;
   " 'tis He fecures my Reign."

9 Preferve thy Chofen, and proceed
   thine Heritage to blefs:
With Plenty profper them in Peace,
   in Battle with Succefs.

PSALM XXIX.

1 YE Princes, that in Might excel,
   your grateful Sacrifice prepare;
God's glorious Actions loudly tell,
   his wondrous Pow'r to all declare.
2 To His great Name fresh Altars raise;
   devoutly due Respect afford;
Him in his holy Temple praise,
   where He's with solemn State ador'd.
3 'Tis He, that with amazing Noise
   the wat'ry Clouds in sunder breaks:
The Ocean trembles at his Voice,
   when He from Heav'n in Thunder speaks.
4, 5 How full of Pow'r his Voice appears!
   with what majestic Terror crown'd!
Which from the Roots tall Cedars tears,
   and strews their scatter'd Branches round.
6 They, and the Hills on which they grow,
   are sometimes hurried far away;
And leap like Hinds that bounding go,
   or Unicorns in youthful Play.
7, 8 When God in Thunder loudly speaks,
   and scatter'd Flames of Lightning sends,
The Forest nods, the Desart quakes,
   and stubborn *Cadesh* lowly bends.
9 He makes the Hind to cast their Young,
   and lays the Beasts' dark Coverts bare;
While those, that to his Courts belong,
   securely sing his Praises there.
10, 11 God rules the angry Floods on high;
   his boundless Sway shall never cease;
His Saints with Strength he will supply,
   and bless his own with constant Peace.

PSALM XXX.

1 I'LL celebrate thy Praises, Lord,
   who didst thy Pow'r employ
To raise my drooping Head, and check
   my Foes, insulting Joy.
2, 3 In my Distress I cry'd to Thee,
   who kindly didst relieve,

PSALM xxx, xxxi.

And from the Grave's expecting Jaws
  my hopeless Life retrieve.
4 Thus to his Courts, ye Saints of his,
  with Songs of Praise repair;
With me commemorate his Truth,
  and Providential Care.
5 His Wrath was but a Moment's Reign,
  his Favour no Decay;
Your Night of Grief is recompens'd
  with Joy's returning Day.
6 But I in prosp'rous Days presum'd;
  no sudden Change I fear'd,
Whilst in my Sunshine of Success
  no lowring Cloud appear'd.
7 But soon I found thy Favour, Lord,
  my Empire's only Trust;
For, when Thou hidd'st thy Face, I saw
  my Honour laid in Dust.
8 Then, as I vainly had presum'd,
  my Error I confess'd;
And thus, with supplicating Voice,
  thy Mercy's Throne address'd:
9 "What Profit is there in my Blood,
  "congeal'd in Death's cold Night?
 "Can silent Ashes speak thy Praise,
  "thy wondrous Truth recite?
10 "Hear me, O Lord, in Mercy hear;
  "thy wonted Aid extend;
 "Do Thou send Help, on whom alone
  "I can for Help depend."
11 'Tis done! Thou hast my mournful Scene
  to Songs and Dances turn'd;
Invested me in Robes of State,
  who late in Sackcloth mourn'd.
12 Exalted thus, I'll gladly sing
  thy Praise in grateful Verse;
And, as thy Favours endless are,
  thy endless Praise rehearse.

PSALM XXXI.

1 DEFEND me, Lord, from Shame;
    for still I trust in Thee:

PSALM xxxi.

As just and righteous is thy Name,
  from Danger set me free.
2 Bow down thy gracious Ear,
  and speedy Succour send:
Do Thou my stedfast Rock appear,
  to shelter and defend.
3 Since Thou, when Foes oppress,
  my Rock and Fortress art,
To guide me forth from this Distress
  thy wonted Help impart.
4 Release me from the Snare,
  which they have closely laid;
Since I, O God, my Strength, repair
  to Thee alone for Aid.
5 To Thee, the God of Truth,
  my Life, and all that's mine,
(For Thou preserv'dst me from my Youth)
  I willingly resign.
6 All vain Designs I hate
  of those that trust in Lies;
And still, my Soul, in ev'ry State,
  to God for Succour flies.

PART II.

7 Those Mercies Thou hast shown,
  I'll cheerfully express;
For Thou hast seen my Streights, and known
  my Soul in deep Distress.
8 When *Keilah's* treach'rous Race
  did all my Strength inclose,
Thou gav'st my Feet a larger Space,
  to shun my watchful Foes.
9 Thy Mercy, Lord, display,
  and hear my just Complaint;
For both my Soul and Flesh decay,
  with Grief and Hunger faint.
10 Sad Thoughts my Life oppress;
  my Years are spent in Groans;
My Sins have made my Strength decrease,
  and ev'n consum'd my Bones.
11 My Foes my Suff'rings mock'd,
  my Neighbours did upbraid;

PSALM xxxi.

  My Friends at Sight of me were shock'd,
   and fled as Men dismay'd.
12 Forsook by all am I,
   as dead and out of Mind;
  And like a shatter'd Vessel lie,
   whose Parts can ne'er be join'd.
13 Yet sland'rous Words they speak,
   and seem my Pow'r to dread;
  Whilst they together Counsel take,
   my guiltless Blood to shed.
14 But still my stedfast Trust
   I on thy Help repose;
  That Thou, my God, art good and just,
   my Soul with Comfort knows.

PART III.

15 Whate'er Events betide,
   thy Wisdom times them all:
  Then, Lord, thy Servant safely hide
   from those that seek his Fall.
16 The Brightness of thy Face
   to me, O Lord, disclose;
  And, as thy Mercies still increase,
   preserve me from my Foes.
17 Me from Dishonour save,
   who still have call'd on Thee:
  Let that, and Silence in the Grave,
   the Sinner's Portion be.
18 Do Thou their Tongues restrain,
   whose Breath in Lies is spent;
  Who false Reports, with proud Disdain,
   against the Righteous vent.
19 How great thy Mercies are
   to such as fear thy Name!
  Which Thou, for those that trust thy Care,
   dost to the World proclaim.
20 Thou keep'st them in thy Sight,
   from proud Oppressors free:
  From Tongues that do in Strife delight,
   they are preserv'd by Thee.
21 With Glory and Renown
   God's Name be ever blest;

          Whose

PSALM xxxi, xxxii.

Whose Love in *Keilah's* well-fenc'd Town
   was wondrously express'd!
22 I said, in hasty Flight,
   " I'm banish'd from thine Eyes;"
   Yet still Thou kept'st me in thy Sight,
   and heard'st my earnest Cries.
23 O! all ye Saints, the Lord
   with eager Love pursue;
   Who to the Just will Help afford,
   and give the Proud their Due.
24 Ye, that on God rely,
   courageously proceed;
   For He will still your Hearts supply
   with Strength in Time of Need.

PSALM XXXII.

1 HE's blest, whose Sins have Pardon gain'd,
   no more in Judgment to appear;
2 Whose Guilt Remission has obtain'd,
   and whose Repentance is sincere.
3 While I conceal'd the fretting Sore,
   my Bones consum'd without Relief:
   All Day did I with Anguish roar,
   but no Complaints assuag'd my Grief.
4 Heavy on me thy Hand remain'd,
   by Day and Night alike distress'd;
   Till quite of vital Moisture drain'd,
   like Land with Summer's Drought oppress'd.
5 No sooner I my Wound disclos'd,
   the Guilt that tortur'd me within,
   But thy Forgiveness interpos'd,
   and Mercy's healing Balm pour'd in.
6 True Penitents shall thus succeed,
   who seek Thee whilst Thou may'st be found;
   And, from the common Deluge freed,
   shall see remorseless Sinners drown'd.
7 Thy Favour, Lord, in all Distress,
   my Tow'r of Refuge I must own:
   Thou shalt my haughty Foes suppress,
   and me with Songs of Triumph crown.
8 In my Instruction then confide,
   you that would Truth's safe Path descry:
                                    Your

Your Progress I'll securely guide,
   and keep you in my watchful Eye.
9 Submit yourselves to Wisdom's Rule,
   like Men that Reason have attain'd;
Not like th' ungovern'd Horse and Mule,
   whose Fury must be curb'd and rein'd.
10 Sorrows, on Sorrows multiply'd,
   the harden'd Sinner shall confound;
But them, who in his Truth confide,
   Blessings of Mercy shall surround.
11 His Saints, that have perform'd his Laws,
   their Life in Triumph shall employ;
Let them (as they alone have Cause)
   in grateful Raptures shout for Joy.

PSALM XXXIII.

1 LET all the Just to God with Joy
   their cheerful Voices raise;
For well the Righteous it becomes
   to sing glad Songs of Praise.
2,3 Let Harps, and Psalteries, and Lutes,
   in joyful Concert meet;
And new-made Songs of loud Applause
   the Harmony complete.
4,5 For faithful is the Word of God;
   his Works with Truth abound;
He Justice loves; and all the Earth
   is with his Goodness crown'd.
6 By his Almighty Word, at first,
   Heav'n's glorious Arch was rear'd;
And all the beauteous Hosts of Light
   at his Command appear'd.
7 The swelling Floods together roll'd
   He makes in Heaps to lie;
And lays, as in a Store-house safe,
   the wat'ry Treasures by.
8,9 Let Earth, and all that dwell therein,
   before Him trembling stand:
For, when He spake the Word, 'twas made;
   'twas fix'd at his Command.
10 He, when the Heathen closely plot,
   their Counsels undermines;

PSALM xxxiii, xxxiv.

His Wisdom ineffectual makes
  the People's rash Designs.
11 Whate'er the mighty Lord decrees
  shall stand for ever sure;
The settled Purpose of his Heart
  to Ages shall endure.

PART II.

12 How happy then are they, to whom
  the Lord for God is known!
Whom He, for all the World besides,
  has chosen for his own.
13,14,15 He all the Nations of the Earth,
  from Heav'n, his Throne, survey'd;
He saw their Works, and view'd their Thoughts;
  by Him their Hearts were made.
16,17 No King is safe by num'rous Hosts;
  their Strength the Strong deceives;
No manag'd Horse by Force or Speed
  his warlike Rider saves.
18,19 'Tis God, who those that trust in Him
  beholds with gracious Eyes:
He frees their Soul from Death; their Want
  in Time of Dearth supplies.
20,21 Our Souls on God with Patience wait;
  our Help and Shield is He:
Then, Lord, let still our Hearts rejoice,
  because we trust in Thee.
22 The Riches of thy Mercy, Lord,
  do Thou to us extend;
Since we, for all we want or wish,
  on Thee alone depend.

PSALM XXXIV.

1 THRO' all the changing Scenes of Life,
    in Trouble and in Joy,
  The Praises of my God shall still
    my Heart and Tongue employ.
2 Of his Deliv'rance I will boast,
    'till all that are distrest,
  From my Example Comfort take,
    and charm their Griefs to Rest.

3 O! magnify the Lord with me,
　　with me exalt his Name:
4 When in Diſtreſs to Him I call'd,
　　He to my Reſcue came.
5 Their drooping Hearts were ſoon refreſh'd,
　　who look'd to Him for Aid:
　Deſir'd Succeſs in ev'ry Face
　　a cheerful Air diſplay'd.
6 " Behold (ſay they) behold the Man
　　" whom Providence reliev'd;
　　" So dang'rouſly with Woes beſet,
　　" ſo wond'rouſly retriev'd!"
7 The Hoſts of God encamp around
　　the Dwellings of the Juſt;
　Deliv'rance He affords to all
　　who on his Succour truſt.
8 O! make but Trial of his Love,
　　Experience will decide
　How bleſt they are, and only they,
　　who in his Truth confide.
9 Fear Him, ye Saints, and you will then
　　have nothing elſe to fear;
　Make you his Service your Delight,
　　He'll make your Wants his Care.
10 While hungry Lions lack their Prey,
　　the Lord will Food provide
　For ſuch as put their Truſt in Him,
　　and ſee their Needs ſupply'd.

PART II.

11 Approach, ye piouſly diſpos'd,
　　and my Inſtructions bear;
　I'll teach you the true Diſcipline
　　of his religious Fear.
12 Let him who Length of Life deſires,
　　and proſp'rous Days would ſee,
13 From ſland'ring Language keep his Tongue,
　　his Lips from Falſehood free.
14 The crooked Paths of Vice decline,
　　and Virtue's Ways purſue:
　Eſtabliſh Peace, where 'tis begun;
　　and, where 'tis loſt, renew.

PSALM xxxiv, xxxv.

15 The Lord from Heav'n beholds the Juſt
  with favourable Eyes;
And, when diſtreſs'd, his gracious Ear
  is open to their Cries;
16 But turns his wrathful Look on thoſe
  whom Mercy can't reclaim,
To cut them off, and from the Earth
  blot out their hated Name.
17 Deliv'rance to his Saints he gives,
  when his Relief they crave:
18 He's nigh to heal the broken Heart,
  and contrite Spirit ſave.
19 The Wicked oft, but ſtill in vain,
  againſt the Juſt conſpire;
20 For under their Affliction's Weight
  He keeps their Bones entire.
21 The Wicked from their wicked Arts
  their Ruin ſhall derive;
Whilſt righteous Men, whom they deteſt,
  ſhall them and theirs ſurvive.
22 For God preſerves the Souls of thoſe,
  who on his Truth depend;
To them and their Poſterity
  his Bleſſings ſhall deſcend.

PSALM XXXV.

1 AGAINST all thoſe that ſtrive with me,
    O Lord, aſſert my Right;
With ſuch as War unjuſtly wage,
  do Thou my Battles fight.
2 Thy Buckler take, and bind thy Shield
  upon thy warlike Arm:
Stand up, my God, in my Defence,
  and keep me ſafe from Harm.
3 Bring forth thy Spear; and ſtop their Courſe,
  that haſte my Blood to ſpill;
Say to my Soul, " I am thy Health,
  " and will preſerve thee ſtill."
4 Let them with Shame be cover'd o'er,
  who my Deſtruction ſought;
And ſuch as did my Harm deviſe,
  be to Confuſion brought.

5 Then

PSALM xxxv.

5 Then shall they fly, dispers'd like Chaff
    before the driving Wind:
God's vengeful Minister of Wrath
    shall follow close behind.
6 And when, through dark and slipp'ry Ways,
    they strive his Rage to shun,
His vengeful Ministers of Wrath
    shall goad them as they run:
7 Since, unprovok'd by any Wrong,
    they hid their treach'rous Snare;
And for my harmless Soul a Pit
    did without Cause prepare:
8 Surpris'd by Mischiefs unforeseen,
    by their own Arts betray'd,
Their Feet shall fall into the Net
    which they for me have laid.
9 Whilst my glad Soul shall God's great Name
    for this Deliv'rance bless;
And, by his saving Health secur'd,
    its grateful Joy express.
10 My very Bones shall say, "O Lord,
    " who can compare with Thee?
" Who sett'st the poor and helpless Man
    " from strong Oppressors free!"

PART II.

11 False Witnesses, with forg'd Complaints,
    against my Truth combin'd;
And to my Charge such Things they laid
    as I had ne'er design'd.
12 The Good which I to them had done
    with Evil they repaid;
And did, by Malice undeserv'd,
    my harmless Life invade.
13 But as for me, when they were sick,
    I still in Sackcloth mourn'd;
I pray'd, and fasted, and my Pray'r
    to my own Breast return'd.
14 Had they my Friends or Brethren been,
    I could have done no more;
Nor with more decent Signs of Grief
    a Mother's Loss deplore.

15 How diff'rent did their Carriage prove,
in Times of my Diſtreſs!
When they, in Crowds together met,
did ſavage Joy expreſs.
The Rabble too, in num'rous Throngs,
by their Example came;
And ceas'd not, with reviling Words,
to wound my ſpotleſs Fame.
16 Scoffers, that noble Tables haunt,
and earn their Bread with Lies,
Did gnaſh their Teeth, and ſland'ring Jeſts
maliciouſly deviſe.
17 But, Lord, how long wilt Thou look on?
on my Behalf appear;
And ſave my guiltleſs Soul, which they
like rav'ning Beaſts would tear.

PART III.

18 So I, before the liſt'ning World,
ſhall grateful Thanks expreſs;
And, where the great Aſſembly meets,
thy Name with Praiſes bleſs.
19 Lord, ſuffer not my cauſeleſs Foes,
who me unjuſtly hate,
With open Joy, or ſecret Signs,
to mock my ſad Eſtate.
20 For they, with Hearts averſe to Peace,
induſtriouſly deviſe
Againſt the Men of quiet Minds
to forge malicious Lies.
21 Nor with theſe private Arts content,
aloud they vent their Spite;
And ſay, " At laſt we found him out,
" he did it in our Sight."
22 But Thou, who doſt both them and me
with righteous Eyes ſurvey,
Aſſert my Innocence, O Lord,
and keep not far away.
23 Stir up Thyſelf in my Behalf;
to Judgment, Lord, awake;
Thy righteous Servant's Cauſe, O God,
to thy Deciſion take.

D   24 Lord,

24 Lord, as my Heart has upright been,
    let me thy Justice find:
Nor let my cruel Foes obtain
    the Triumphs they design'd.
25 O! let them not, amongst themselves,
    in boasting Language say,
"At length our Wishes are complete;
"at last he's made our Prey."
26 Let such as in my Harm rejoic'd,
    for Shame their Faces hide;
And foul Dishonour wait on those
    that proudly me defy'd.
27 Whilst they with cheerful Voices shout,
    who my just Cause befriend:
And bless the Lord, who loves to make
    success his Saints attend.
28 So shall my Tongue thy Judgments sing,
    inspir'd with grateful Joy;
And cheerful Hymns of Praise to Thee
    shall all my Days employ.

PSALM XXXVI.

1 MY crafty Foe, with flatt'ring Art,
    his wicked Purpose would disguise:
But Reason whispers to my Heart,
    no Fear of God's before his Eyes.
2 He sooths himself, retir'd from Sight,
    secure he thinks his treach'rous Game:
Till his dark Plots, expos'd to Light,
    their false Contriver brand with Shame.
3 In Deeds he is my Foe confess'd,
    whilst with his Tongue he speaks me fair:
True Wisdom's banish'd from his Breast,
    and Vice has sole Dominion there.
4 His wakeful Malice spends the Night
    in forging his accurs'd Designs;
His obstinate, ungen'rous Spite
    no execrable Means declines.
5 But, Lord, thy Mercy, my sure Hope,
    the highest Orb of Heav'n transcends;
Thy sacred Truth's unmeasur'd Scope
    beyond the spreading Sky extends.

PSALM xxxvi, xxxvii.

6 Thy Justice like the Hills remains;
    unfathom'd Depths thy Judgments are;
Thy Providence the World sustains;
    the whole Creation is thy Care.
7 Since of thy Goodness all partake,
    with what Assurance should the Just
Thy shelt'ring Wings their Refuge make,
    and Saints to thy Protection trust.
8 Such Guests shall to thy Courts be led,
    to banquet on thy Love's Repast;
And drink, as from a Fountain's Head,
    of Joys that shall for ever last.
9 With Thee the Springs of Life remain;
    thy Presence is eternal Day:
10 O! let thy Saints thy Favour gain;
    to upright Hearts thy Truth display.
11 Whilst Pride's insulting Foot would spurn,
    and wicked Hand my Life surprise;
12 Their Mischief on themselves return;
    down, down they're fall'n, no more to rise.

PSALM XXXVII.

1 THO' wicked Men grow rich or great,
    Yet let not their successful State
thy Anger or thy Envy raise;
2. For they, cut down like tender Grass,
Or, like young Flow'rs, away shall pass,
    whose blooming Beauty soon decays.
3 Depend on God, and Him obey;
So thou within the Land shalt stay,
    secure from Danger and from Want:
4. Make his Commands thy chief Delight,
And He, thy Duty to requite,
    shall all thy earnest Wishes grant.
5 In all thy Ways trust thou the Lord,
And He will needful Help afford
    to perfect ev'ry just Design;
6 He'll make, like Light serene and clear,
Thy clouded Innocence appear,
    and as a mid-day Sun to shine.
7 With quiet Mind on God depend,
And patiently for Him attend;
    nor let thy Anger fondly rise,

PSALM xxxvii.

Tho' wicked Men with Wealth abound,
And with Success the Plots are crown'd,
  which they maliciously devise.
8 From Anger cease, and Wrath forsake;
Let no ungovern'd Passion make
  thy wav'ring Heart espouse their Crime;
9 For God shall sinful Men destroy;
Whilst only they the Land enjoy,
  who trust in Him and wait his Time.
10 How soon shall wicked Men decay!
Their Place shall vanish quite away,
  nor by the strictest Search be found;
11 Whilst humble Souls possess the Earth,
Rejoicing still with godly Mirth,
  with Peace and Plenty always crown'd.

PART II.

12 Whilst sinful Crowds, with false Design,
Against the righteous Few combine,
  and gnash their Teeth and threat'ning stand;
13 God shall their empty Plots deride,
And laugh at their defeated Pride:
  He sees their Ruin near at Hand.
14 They draw the Sword, and bend the Bow,
The Poor and Needy to o'erthrow,
  and Men of upright Lives to slay;
15 But their strong Bows shall soon be broke,
Their sharpen'd Weapon's mortal Stroke
  thro' their own Hearts shall force its Way.
16 A little, with God's Favour bless'd,
That's by one righteous Man possess'd,
  the Wealth of many bad excels:
17 For God supports the just Man's Cause;
But as for those that break his Laws,
  their unsuccessful Pow'r He quells.
18 His constant Care the Upright guides,
And over all their Life presides;
  their Portion shall for ever last:
19 They, when Distress o'erwhelms the Earth,
Shall be unmov'd, and even in Dearth
  the happy Fruits of Plenty taste.

20 Not

PSALM xxxvii.

20 Not so the wicked Man, and those
Who proudly dare God's Will oppose:
  Destruction is their hapless Share:
  Like Fat of Lambs, their Hopes, and they,
  Shall in an Instant melt away,
    and vanish into Smoke and Air.

PART III.

21 While Sinners, brought to sad Decay,
Still borrow on, and never pay,
  the Just have Will and Pow'r to give:
22 For such, as God vouchsafes to bless,
Shall peaceably the Earth possess;
  and those He curses shall not live.
23 The good Man's Way is God's Delight;
He orders all the Steps aright
  of him that moves by his Command:
24 Though he sometimes may be distress'd,
Yet shall he ne'er be quite oppress'd;
  for God upholds him with his Hand.
25 From my first Youth, till Age prevail'd,
I never saw the Righteous fail'd,
  or Want o'ertake his num'rous Race;
26 Because Compassion fill'd his Heart,
And he did cheerfully impart,
  God made his Offspring's Wealth increase.
27 With Caution shun each wicked Deed,
In Virtue's Ways with Zeal proceed,
  and so prolong your happy Days:
28 For God, who Judgment loves, does still
Preserve his Saints secure from Ill,
  while soon the wicked Race decays.
29,30,31 The Upright shall possess the Land;
His Portion shall for Ages stand,
  his Mouth with Wisdom is supply'd:
  His Tongue by Rules of Judgment moves;
  His Heart the Law of God approves;
    therefore his Footsteps never slide.

PART IV.

32 In Wait the watchful Sinner lies,
In vain the Righteous to surprise;
  in vain his Ruin doth decree:

PSALM xxxvii, xxxviii.

33 God will not him defenceless leave,
   To his Revenge expos'd, but save;
      and, when he's sentenc'd, set him free.
34 Wait still on God; keep his Command;
   And thou, exalted in the Land,
      thy blest Possession ne'er shalt quit:
   The wicked soon destroy'd shall be,
   And at his dismal Tragedy
      thou shalt a safe Spectator sit.
35 The Wicked I in Pow'r have seen,
   And, like a Bay-Tree fresh and green,
      that spreads its pleasant Branches round;
36 But he was gone as swift as Thought,
   And, tho' in ev'ry Place I sought,
      no Sign or Track of him I found.
37 Observe the perfect Man with Care,
   And mark all such as upright are;
      their roughest Days in Peace shall end;
38 While on the latter End of those,
   Who dare God's sacred Will oppose,
      a common Ruin shall attend.
39 God to the Just will Aid afford:
   Their only Safeguard is the Lord;
      their Strength in Time of Need is He;
40 Because on Him they still depend,
   The Lord will timely Succour send,
      and from the Wicked set them free.

PSALM XXXVIII.

1 THY chast'ning Wrath, O Lord, restrain,
      tho' I deserve it all;
   Nor let at once on me the Storm
      of thy Displeasure fall.
2 In ev'ry wretched Part of me
      thy Arrows deep remain;
   Thy heavy Hand's afflicting Weight
      I can no more sustain.
3 My Flesh is one continu'd Wound,
      thy Wrath so fiercely glows;
   Betwixt my Punishment and Guilt
      my Bones have no Repose.
4 My Sins, which to a Deluge swell,
      my sinking Head o'erflow;

And,

PSALM xxxviii.

And, for my feeble Strength to bear,
  too vast a Burthen grow.
5 Stench and Corruption fill my Wounds,
  my Folly's just Return:
6 With Troubles I am warp'd and bow'd,
  and all Day long I mourn.
7 A loath'd Disease afflicts my Loins,
  infecting ev'ry Part;
8 With Sickness worn I groan and roar
  thro' Anguish of my Heart.
9 But, Lord, before thy searching Eyes
  all my Desires appear;
And sure my Groans have been too loud
  not to have reach'd thine Ear.
10 My Heart's oppress'd, my Strength decay'd,
  my Eyes depriv'd of Light:
11 Friends, Lovers, Kinsmen, gaze aloof
  on such a dismal Sight.
12 Mean while, the Foes that seek my Life
  their Snares to take me set;
Vent Slanders, and contrive all Day
  to forge some new Deceit.
13 But I, as if both deaf and dumb,
  nor heard, nor once reply'd:
14 Quite deaf and dumb, like one whose Tongue
  with conscious Guilt is ty'd.
15 For, Lord, to thee I do appeal,
  my Innocence to clear;
Assur'd that Thou, the righteous God,
  my injur'd Cause wilt hear.
16 " Hear me," said I, " lest my proud Foes
  " a spiteful Joy display;
  " Insulting, if they see my Foot
  " but once to go astray."
17 And, with continual Grief oppress'd,
  to sink I now begin:
18 To Thee, O Lord, I will confess,
  to Thee bewail my Sin.
19 But whilst I languish, my proud Foes
  their Strength and Vigour boast;
And they, who hate me without Cause,
  are grown a dreadful Host.

D 4   20 Ev'n

20 Ev'n they, whom I oblig'd, return
    my Kindness with Despite;
  And are my Enemies, because
    I choose the Path that's right.
21 Forsake me not, O Lord, my God,
    nor far from me depart;
22 Make haste to my Relief, O Thou,
    who my Salvation art.

PSALM XXXIX.

1 REsolv'd to watch o'er all my Ways,
    I kept my Tongue in Awe;
  I curb'd my hasty Words, when I
    the Wicked prosp'rous saw.
2 Like one that's dumb, I silent stood,
    and did my Tongue refrain
  From good Discourse; but that Restraint
    increas'd my inward Pain.
3 My Heart did glow, which working Thoughts
    did hot and restless make;
  And warm Reflections fann'd the Fire,
    till thus at length I spake:
4 Lord, let me know my Term of Days,
    how soon my Life will end;
  The num'rous Train of Ills disclose,
    which this frail state attend.
5 My Life thou know'st is but a Span,
    a Cypher sums my Years;
  And ev'ry Man, in best Estate,
    but Vanity appears.
6 Man, like a Shadow, vainly walks,
    with fruitless Cares oppress'd:
  He heaps up Wealth, but cannot tell
    by whom 'twill be possess'd.
7 Why should I then on worthless Toys
    with anxious Care attend?
  On Thee alone my stedfast Hope
    shall ever, Lord, depend.
8,9 Forgive my Sins; nor let me scorn'd
    by foolish Sinners be;
  For I was dumb, and murmur'd not,
    because 'twas done by Thee.

10 The dreadful Burthen of thy Wrath
  in Mercy soon remove;
 Lest my frail Flesh too weak to bear
  the heavy Load should prove.
11 For when thou chast'nest Man for Sin,
  thou mak'st his Beauty fade
 (So vain a Thing is he!) like Cloth
  by fretting Moths decay'd.
12 Lord, hear my Cry, accept my Tears,
  and listen to my Pray'r;
 Who sojourn like a Stranger here,
  as all my Fathers were.
13 O spare me yet a little Time,
  my wasted Strength restore,
 Before I vanish quite from hence,
  And shall be seen no more.

PSALM XL.

1 I Waited meekly for the Lord,
   till He vouchsaf'd a kind reply:
 Who did his gracious Ear afford,
   and heard from Heav'n my humble Cry.
2 He took me from the dismal Pit,
   when founder'd deep in miry Clay;
 On solid Ground He plac'd my Feet,
   and suffer'd not my Steps to stray.
3 The Wonders He for me has wrought
   shall fill my Mouth with Songs of Praise;
 And others, to his Worship brought,
   to Hopes of like Deliv'rance raise.
4 For Blessings shall that Man reward,
   who on th' Almighty Lord relies;
 Who treats the Proud with Disregard,
   and hates the Hypocrite's Disguise.
5 Who can the wond'rous Works recount
   which Thou, O God, for us hast wrought?
 The Treasures of thy Love surmount
   the Pow'r of Numbers, Speech, and Thought.
6 I've learnt that Thou hast not desir'd
   Off'rings and Sacrifice alone:
 Nor Blood of guiltless Beasts requir'd,
   for Man's Transgression to atone.

7 I therefore come—come to fulfil
  the Oracles thy Books impart:
8 'Tis my Delight to do thy Will;
  thy Law is written in my Heart.

PART II.

9 In full Assemblies I have told
  thy Truth and Righteousness at large:
  Nor did, Thou know'st, my Lips with-hold
  from utt'ring what Thou gav'st in Charge;
10 Nor kept within my Breast confin'd
  thy Faithfulness and saving Grace;
  But preach'd thy Love, for All design'd,
  that All might that and Truth embrace.
11 Then let those Mercies I declar'd
  to others, Lord, extend to me:
  Thy Loving-kindness my Reward,
  thy Truth my safe Protection be.
12 For I with Troubles am distress'd,
  too vast and numberless to bear;
  Nor less with Loads of Guilt oppress'd,
  that plunge and sink me to Despair.
  As soon, alas! I may recount
  the Hairs on this afflicted Head;
  My vanquish'd Courage they surmount,
  and fill my drooping Soul with Dread.

PART III.

13 But, Lord, to my Relief draw near,
  for never was more pressing Need;
  In my Deliv'rance, Lord, appear,
  and add to that Deliv'rance Speed.
14 Confusion on their Heads return,
  who to destroy my Soul combine;
  Let them defeated, blush and mourn,
  ensnar'd in their own vile Design.
15 Their Doom let Desolation be,
  with Shame their Malice be repaid,
  Who mock'd my Confidence in Thee,
  and Sport of my Affliction made:
16 While they, who humbly seek thy Face,
  to joyful Triumphs shall be rais'd:

And

PSALM xl, xli.

And all who prize thy saving Grace
  with me refound, The Lord be prais'd.
17 Thus, wretched tho' I am, and poor,
  of me th' Almighty Lord takes Care:
Thou, God, who only canft reftore,
  to my Relief with Speed repair.

PSALM XLI.

1 HAPPY the Man, whofe tender Care
  relieves the Poor diftrefs'd:
When Troubles compafs him around,
  the Lord fhall give him Reft.
2 The Lord his Life, with Bleffings crown'd,
  in Safety fhall prolong;
And difappoint the Will of thofe
  that feek to do him Wrong.
3 If he in languifhing Eftate,
  opprefs'd with Sicknefs, lie;
The Lord will eafy make his Bed,
  and inward Strength fupply.
4 Secure of this, to Thee, my God,
  I thus my Pray'r addrefs'd:
" Lord, for thy Mercy, heal my Soul,
" tho' I have much tranfgrefs'd."
5 My cruel Foes with fland'ring Words
  attempt to wound my Fame:
" When fhall he die (fay they) and Men
" forget his very Name?"
6 Suppofe they formal Vifits make,
  'tis all but empty Show;
They gather Mifchief in their Hearts,
  and vent it where they go.
7, 8 With private Whifpers, fuch as thefe,
  to hurt me they devife:
" A fore Difeafe afflicts him now;
" he's fall'n, no more to rife."
9 My own familiar Bofom-Friend,
  on whom I moft rely'd,
Has me, whofe daily Gueft he was,
  with open Scorn defy'd.
10 But Thou, my fad and wretched State,
  in Mercy, Lord, regard;

And

PSALM xli, xlii.

And raise me up, that all their Crimes
may meet their just Reward.
11 By this I know thy gracious Ear
is open when I call;
Because Thou suffer'st not my Foes
to triumph in my Fall.
12 Thy tender Care secures my Life
from Danger and Disgrace;
And Thou vouchsaf'st to set me still
before thy glorious Face.
13 Let therefore *Israel's* Lord and God
from Age to Age be blest;
And all the People's glad Applause
with loud Amens exprest.

PSALM XLII.

1 AS pants the Hart for cooling Streams,
when heated in the Chace;
So longs my Soul, O God, for Thee
and thy refreshing Grace.
2 For Thee, my God, the living God,
my thirsty Soul doth pine;
O! when shall I behold thy Face,
thou Majesty Divine!
3 Tears are my constant Food, while thus
insulting Foes upbraid:
"Deluded Wretch! where's now thy God?
"And where his promis'd Aid?"
4 I sigh whene'er my musing Thoughts
those happy Days present,
When I, with Troops of pious Friends,
thy Temple did frequent:
When I advanc'd with Songs of Praise,
my solemn Vows to pay;
And led the joyful sacred Throng
that kept the Festal Day.
5 Why restless, why cast down, my Soul?
trust God; and He'll employ
His Aid for thee, and change these Sighs
to thankful Hymns of Joy.
6 My Soul's cast down, O God! but thinks
on Thee and *Sion* still:

From

PSALM xlii, xliii.

From *Jordan's* Banks, from *Hermon's* Heights,
  and *Mizar's* humbler Hill.
7 One Trouble calls another on ;
  and bursting o'er my Head,
Fall spouting down, till round my Soul
  a roaring Sea is spread.
8 But when thy Presence, Lord of Life,
  has once dispell'd this Storm,
To Thee I'll midnight Anthems sing,
  and all my Vows perform.
9 God of my Strength, how long shall I
  like one forgotten mourn ?
Forlorn, forsaken, and expos'd
  to my Oppressor's Scorn.
10 My Heart is pierc'd as with a Sword,
  whilst thus my Foes upbraid,
" Vain Boaster, where is now thy God ?
" And where his promis'd Aid ?"
11 Why restless, why cast down, my Soul ?
  hope still ; and thou shalt sing
The Praise of Him who is thy God,
  thy Health's eternal Spring.

PSALM XLIII.

1 JUST Judge of Heav'n, against my Foes
  do Thou assert my injur'd Right :
O ! set me free, my God, from those,
  that in Deceit and Wrong delight.
2 Since Thou art still my only Stay,
  why leav'st Thou me in deep Distress ?
Why go I mourning all the Day,
  whilst me insulting Foes oppress.
3 Let me with Light and Truth be blest ;
  be these my Guides, and lead the Way,
Till on thy holy Hill I rest,
  and in thy sacred Temple pray.
4 Then will I there fresh Altars raise
  to God, who is my only Joy :
And well-tun'd Harps, with Songs of Praise,
  shall all my grateful Hours employ.
5 Why then cast down, my Soul ? And why
  so much oppress'd with anxious Care ?

On God, thy God, for Aid rely,
   who will thy ruin'd State repair.

PSALM XLIV.

1 O LORD, our Fathers oft have told,
   in our attentive Ears,
Thy Wonders in their Days perform'd,
   and elder Times than theirs.
2 How Thou, to plant them here, did'st drive
   the Heathen from this Land,
Difpeopled by repeated Strokes
   of thy avenging Hand.
3 For, not their Courage, nor their Sword,
   to them Poffeffion gave;
Nor Strength, that from unequal Force
   their fainting Troops could fave.
But thy Right-hand and pow'rful Arm,
   whofe Succour they implor'd;
Thy Prefence with the chofen Race,
   who thy great Name ador'd.
4 As Thee, their God, our Fathers own'd;
   Thou art our Sov'reign King;
O! therefore, as Thou did'st to them,
   to us Deliv'rance bring.
5 Through thy victorious Name our Arms
   the proudeft Foes fhall quell;
And crufh them with repeated Strokes
   as oft as they rebel.
6 I'll neither truft my Bow nor Sword,
   when I in Fight engage;
7 But Thee, who haft our Foes fubdu'd,
   and fham'd their fpiteful Rage.
8 To Thee the Triumph we afcribe,
   from whence the Conqueft came:
In God we will rejoice all Day,
   and ever blefs his Name.

PART II.

9 But Thou haft caft us off; and now
   moft fhamefully we yield;
For Thou no more vouchfaf'ft to lead
   our Armies to the Field.

10 Since when, to ev'ry upstart Foe
  we turn our backs in Fight;
 And with our Spoil their Malice feast
  who bear us antient Spite.
11 To slaughter doom'd, we fall, like Sheep,
  into their butch'ring Hands;
 Or (what's more wretched yet) survive,
  dispers'd thro' Heathen Lands.
12 Thy People thou hast sold for Slaves;
  and set their Price so low,
 That not thy Treasure by the Sale
  but their Disgrace might grow.
13, 14 Reproach'd by all the Nations round,
  the Heathens By-word grown;
 Whose Scorn of us is both in Speech
  and mocking Gestures shown.
15 Confusion strikes me blind; my Face
  in conscious Shame I hide;
16 While we are scoff'd, and God blasphem'd,
  by their licentious Pride.

PART III.

17 On us this Heap of Woe is fall'n;
  all this we have endur'd:
 Yet have not, Lord, renounc'd thy Name,
  or Faith to thee abjur'd:
18 But in thy righteous Paths have kept
  our Hearts and Steps with Care;
19 Tho' Thou hast broken all our Strength,
  and we almost despair.
20 Could we, forgetting thy great Name,
  on other Gods rely,
21 And not the Searcher of all Hearts
  the treach'rous Crime descry?
22 Thou seest what Suff'rings for thy Sake
  we ev'ry Day sustain;
 All slaughter'd or reserv'd like Sheep
  appointed to be slain.
23 Awake, arise; let seeming Sleep
  no longer Thee detain;
 Nor let us, Lord, who sue to Thee,
  for ever sue in vain.

24 O!

24 O! wherefore hidest Thou thy Face
   from our afflicted State,
25 Whose Souls and Bodies sink to Earth
   with Grief's oppressive Weight?
26 Arise, O Lord, and timely Haste
   to our Deliv'rance make:
   Redeem us, Lord; if not for ours,
   yet for thy Mercy's sake.

PSALM XLV.

1 WHILE I the King's loud Praise rehearse,
    indited by my Heart,
  My Tongue is like the Pen of Him
    that writes with ready Art.
2 How matchless is thy Form, O King!
    thy Mouth with Grace o'erflows;
  Because fresh Blessings God on thee
    eternally bestows.
3 Gird on thy Sword, most mighty Prince;
    and, clad in rich Array,
  With glorious Ornaments of Pow'r,
    majestic Pomp display.
4 Ride on in State, and still protect
    the Meek, the Just, and True;
  Whilst thy Right-hand, with swift Revenge,
    does all thy Foes pursue.
5 How sharp thy Weapons are to them
    that dare thy Pow'r oppose!
  Down, down they fall, while thro' their Heart
    the feather'd Arrow goes.
6 But thy firm Throne, O God, is fix'd,
    for ever to endure:
  Thy Sceptre's Sway shall always last,
    by righteous Laws secure.
7 Because thy Heart, by Justice led,
    did upright Ways approve,
  And hated still the crooked Paths,
    where wand'ring Sinners rove;
  Therefore did God, thy God, on thee
    the Oil of Gladness shed;
  And has, above thy Fellows round,
    advanc'd thy lofty Head.

PSALM xlv.

8 With Caffia, Alöes, and Myrrh,
    thy royal Robes abound;
 Which, from the stately Wardrobe brought,
    spread grateful Odours round.
9 Among the honourable Train
    did princely Virgins wait;
 The Queen was plac'd at thy Right-hand
    in golden Robes of State.

PART II.

10 But thou, O royal Bride, give Ear,
    and to my Words attend;
 Forget thy native Country now,
    and ev'ry former Friend:
11 So shall thy Beauty charm the King,
    nor shall his Love decay!
 For he is now become thy Lord:
    to him due Rev'rence pay.
12 The *Tyrian* Matrons, rich and proud,
    shall humble Presents make;
 And all the wealthy Nations sue
    thy Favour to partake.
13 The King's fair Daughter's beauteous Soul
    all inward Graces fill:
 Her Raiment is of purest Gold,
    adorn'd with costly Skill.
14 She, in her Nuptial Garments dress'd,
    with Needles richly wrought,
 Attended by her Virgin Train,
    shall to the King be brought.
15 With all the State of solemn Joy
    the Triumph moves along,
 'Till, with wide Gates, the royal Court
    receives the pompous Throng.
16 Thou, in thy Royal Father's Room,
    must princely Sons expect;
 Whom Thou to diff'rent Realms may'st send
    to govern and protect.
17 Whilst this my Song to future Times
    transmits thy Glorious Name;
 And makes the World, with one Consent,
    thy lasting Praise proclaim.

PSALM XLVI.

1 GOD is our Refuge in Diſtreſs;
   A preſent Help when Dangers preſs;
   in Him, undaunted, we'll confide;
2,3, Tho' Earth were from her Centre toſt,
   And Mountains in the Ocean loſt,
   torn Piece-meal by the roaring Tide.
4 A gentler Stream with Gladneſs ſtill
   The City of our Lord ſhall fill,
   the royal Seat of God moſt High.
5 God dwells in *Sion*, whoſe fair Tow'rs
   Shall mock th' Aſſaults of earthly Pow'rs,
   while his Almighty Aid is nigh.
6 In Tumults when the Heathen rag'd,
   And Kingdoms War againſt us wag'd,
   He thunder'd, and diſpers'd their Pow'rs.
7 The Lord of Hoſts conducts our Arms,
   Our Tow'r of Refuge in Alarms,
   our Fathers' Guardian-God and ours.
8 Come, ſee the Wonders He has wrought,
   On Earth what Deſolation brought;
   how he has calm'd the jarring World,
9 He broke the warlike Spear and Bow;
   With them, their thund'ring Chariots too
   into devouring Flames were hurl'd.
10 Submit to God's Almighty Sway;
   For, Him the Heathen ſhall obey,
   and Earth her Sov'reign Lord confeſs.
11 The Lord of Hoſts conducts our Arms,
   Our Tow'r of Refuge in Alarms,
   as to our Fathers in Diſtreſs.

PSALM XLVII.

1,2 O All ye People, clap your Hands,
     and with triumphant Voices ſing.
   No Force the mighty Pow'r withſtands
   of God, the Univerſal King.
3,4 He ſhall oppoſing Nations quell,
    and with Succeſs our Battles fight;
   Shall fix the Place where we muſt dwell,
   the Pride of *Jacob* his Delight.

5,6 God

5,6 God is gone up, our Lord and King,
    with Shouts of Joy, and Trumpets' Sound:
To him repeated Praises sing,
    and let the cheerful Song go round.
7,8 Your utmost Skill in Praise be shown
    for Him, who all the World commands,
Who sits upon his righteous Throne,
    and spreads his Sway o'er Heathen Lands.
9 Our Chiefs and Tribes, that far from hence
    t' adore the God of *Abr'am* came,
Found him their constant sure Defence:
    how great and glorious is his Name!

PSALM XLVIII.

1 THE Lord, the only God, is great,
    and greatly to be prais'd
In *Sion*, on whose happy Mount
    his sacred Throne is rais'd.
2 Her Tow'rs, the Joy of all the Earth,
    with beauteous Prospect rise:
On her North Side th' Almighty King's
    imperial City lies.
3 God in her Palaces is known;
    his Presence is her Guard.
4 Confed'rate Kings withdrew their Siege,
    and of Success despair'd:
5 They view'd her Walls, admir'd, and fled,
    with Grief and Terror struck,
6 Like Women, whom the sudden Pangs
    of Travail had o'ertook:
7 No wretched Crew of Mariners
    appear like them forlorn,
When Fleets from *Tarshish* wealthy Coasts
    by Eastern Winds are torn.
8 In *Sion* we have seen perform'd
    a Work that was foretold,
In Pledge that God, for Times to come,
    his City will uphold.
9 Not in our Fortresses and Walls
    did we, O God, confide;
But on the Temple fix'd our Hopes
    in which thou dost reside.

10 According

10 According to thy Sov'reign Name,
  thy Praise thro' Earth extends;
  Thy pow'rful Arm, as Justice guides,
  chastises or defends.
11 Let *Sion's* Mount with Joy resound;
  her Daughters all be taught
  In Songs his Judgments to extol
  who this Deliv'rance wrought.
12 Compass her Walls in solemn Pomp;
  your Eyes quite round her cast;
  Count all her Tow'rs, and see if there
  you find one Stone displac'd:
13 Her Forts and Palaces survey;
  observe their Order well;
  That, with Assurance, to your Heirs
  this Wonder you may tell.
14 This God is ours, and will be ours,
  whilst we in Him confide;
  Who, as He has preserv'd us now,
  till Death will be our Guide.

PSALM XLIX.

1,2 LET all the list'ning World attend,
  and my Instructions hear:
  Let High and Low, and Rich and Poor,
  with joint Consent give Ear.
3 My Mouth, with sacred Wisdom fill'd,
  shall good Advice impart,
  The sound Result of prudent Thoughts
  digested in my Heart.
4 To Parables of weighty Sense
  I will my Ear incline;
  While to my tuneful Harp I sing
  dark Words of deep Design.
5 Why should my Courage fail in Times
  of Danger and of Doubt;
  When Sinners, that would me supplant,
  have compass'd me about?
6 Those Men, that all their Hope and Trust
  in Heaps of Treasure place,
  And boast in Triumph when they see
  their ill-got Wealth increase,

7 Are

PSALM xlix.

7 Are yet unable from the Grave
   their dearest Friend to free;
   Nor can, by Force of costly Bribes,
   reverse God's firm Decree.
8,9 Their vain Endeavours they must quit;
   the Price is held too high:
   No Sum can purchase such a Grant,
   that Man should never die.
10 Not Wisdom can the Wise exempt,
   nor Fools their Folly save;
   But both must perish, and, in Death,
   their Wealth to others leave;
11 For, tho' they think their stately Seats
   shall ne'er to Ruin fall;
   But their Remembrance last, in Lands
   which by their Names they call;
12 Yet shall their Fame be soon forgot,
   how great soe'er their State:
   With Beasts their Memory and they
   shall share one common Fate.

PART II.

13 How great their Folly is, who thus
   absurd Conclusions make!
   And yet their Children, unreclaim'd,
   repeat the gross Mistake.
14 They all, like Sheep to Slaughter led,
   the Prey of Death are made;
   Their Beauty, while the Just rejoice,
   within the Grave shall fade.
15 But God will yet redeem my Soul;
   and from the greedy Grave
   His greater Pow'r shall set me free,
   and to Himself receive.
16 Then fear not thou, when worldly Men
   in envy'd Wealth abound;
   Nor, tho' their prosp'rous House increase,
   with State and Honour crown'd;
17 For, when they're summon'd hence by Death,
   they leave all this behind:
   No Shadow of their former Pomp
   within the Grave they find.

18 And yet they thought their State was bleſt,
  caught in the Flatt'rer's Snare,
 Who praiſes thoſe that ſlight all elſe,
  and of themſelves take Care.
19 In their Forefathers' Steps they tread,
  and when, like them, they die,
 Their wretched Anceſtors and they
  in endleſs Darkneſs lie:
20 For Man, how great ſoe'er his State,
  unleſs he's truly wiſe,
 As like a ſenſual Beaſt he lives,
  ſo like a Beaſt he dies.

PSALM L.

1,2 THE Lord hath ſpoke; the mighty God
  hath ſent His Summons all abroad,
 from dawning Light till Day declines:
 The liſt'ning Earth His Voice hath heard,
 And He from *Sion* hath appear'd,
  where Beauty in Perfection ſhines.
3,4 Our God ſhall come, and keep no more
 Miſconſtru'd Silence, as before;
  but waſting Flames before Him ſend:
 Around ſhall Tempeſts fiercely rage,
 While He does Heav'n and Earth engage
  His juſt Tribunal to attend.
5,6 Aſſemble all my Saints to Me
 (Thus runs the great Divine Decree)
  that in my laſting Cov'nant live;
 And Off'rings bring with conſtant Care
 (The Heav'ns his Juſtice ſhall declare,
  for God himſelf ſhall Sentence give).
7 Attend, my People: *Iſrael*, hear:
 Thy ſtrong Accuſer I'll appear;
  thy God, thy only God, am I:
8 'Tis not of Off'rings I complain,
 Which, daily in my Temple ſlain,
  my ſacred Altar did ſupply.
9 Will this alone Atonement make?
 No Bullock from thy Stall I'll take,
  nor He-goat from thy Fold accept;

PSALM l.

10 The Forest-beasts, that range alone,
　The Cattle too, are all my own,
　　that on a thousand Hills are kept.
11 I know the Fowls that build their Nests
　In craggy Rocks, and savage Beasts
　　that loosely haunt the open Fields:
12 If seiz'd with Hunger I could be,
　I need not seek Relief from thee,
　　since the World's mine, and all it yields.
13 Think'st thou that I have any Need
　On slaughter'd Bulls and Goats to feed,
　　to eat their Flesh and drink their Blood?
14 The Sacrifices I require
　Are Hearts which Love and Zeal inspire,
　　and Vows with strictest Care made good.
15 In Time of Trouble call on Me,
　And I will set thee safe and free;
　　and thou Returns of Praise shalt make:
16 But to the Wicked thus saith God,
　How dar'st thou teach my Laws abroad,
　　or in thy Mouth my Cov'nant take?
17 For stubborn thou, confirm'd in Sin,
　Hast Proof against Instruction been,
　　and of my Word didst lightly speak.
18 When thou a subtle Thief didst see,
　Thou gladly didst with him agree,
　　and with Adult'rers didst partake:
19 Vile Slander is thy chief Delight;
　Thy Tongue, by Envy mov'd, and Spite,
　　deceitful Tales does hourly spread:
20 Thou dost with hateful Scandal wound
　Thy Brother, and with Lies confound
　　the Offspring of thy Mother's Bed:
21 These Things didst thou: whom still I strove
　To gain with silence and with Love,
　　till thou didst wickedly surmise,
　That I was such an one as thou:
　But I'll reprove and shame thee now,
　　and set thy Sins before thine Eyes.
22 Mark this, ye wicked Fools, lest I
　Let all my Bolts of Vengeance fly,
　　while none shall dare your Cause to own.

23 Who praises me due Honour gives;
  And to the Man that justly lives
   my strong Salvation shall be shown.

PSALM LI.

1 HAVE Mercy, Lord, on me,
   as Thou wert ever kind;
  Let me, oppress'd with Loads of Guilt,
   thy wonted Mercy find.
2, 3 Wash off my foul Offence,
   and cleanse me from my Sin;
  For, I confess my Crime, and see
   how great my Guilt has been.
4 Against Thee, Lord, alone,
   and only in thy Sight,
  Have I transgress'd; and, tho' condemn'd,
   must own thy Judgments right.
5 In Guilt each Part was form'd
   of all this sinful Frame;
  In Guilt I was conceiv'd and born,
   the Heir of Sin and Shame.
6 Yet thou, whose searching Eye
   does inward Truth require,
  In Secret didst with Wisdom's Laws
   my tender Soul inspire.
7 With Hyssop purge me, Lord,
   and so I clean shall be;
  I shall with Snow in Whiteness vie,
   when purify'd by Thee.
8 Make me to hear with Joy
   thy kind forgiving Voice;
  That to my Bones, which thou hast broke,
   may with fresh Strength rejoice.
9, 10 Blot out my crying Sins,
   nor me in Anger view;
  Create in me a Heart that's clean,
   an upright Mind renew.

PART II.

11 Withdraw not Thou thy Help,
   nor cast me from thy Sight;
  Nor let thy Holy Spirit take
   its everlasting Flight.

PSALM li, lii.

12 The Joy thy Favour gives
  let me again obtain!
And let thy Spirit's firm Support
  my fainting Soul suſtain:
13 So I thy righteous Ways
  to Sinners will impart;
While my Advice ſhall wicked Men
  to thy juſt Laws convert.
14 My Guilt of Blood remove,
  my Saviour and my God;
And my glad Tongue ſhall loudly tell
  Thy righteous Acts abroad.
15 Do Thou unlock my Lips,
  with Sorrow clos'd and Shame;
So ſhall my Mouth thy wond'rous Praiſe
  to all the World proclaim.
16 Could Sacrifice atone,
  whole Flocks and Lerds ſhould die;
But on ſuch Off'rings Thou diſdain'ſt
  to caſt a gracious Eye:
17 A broken Sp rit is
  by God moſt highly priz'd;
By Him a broken contrite Heart
  ſhall never be deſpis'd.
18 Let Sion Favour find,
  of thy Good-will aſſur'd;
And thy own City flouriſh long,
  by lofty Walls ſecur'd.
19 The Juſt ſhall then attend,
  and pleaſing Tribute pay;
And Sacrifice of choiceſt Kind
  upon thy Altar lay.

PSALM LII.

1. IN vain, O Man of lawleſs Might,
    thou boaſt'ſt thyſelf in Ill;
  Since God, the God in whom I truſt,
    vouchſafes his Favour ſtill.
2 Thy wicked Tongue doth ſland'rous Tales
    maliciouſly deviſe,
  And, ſharper than a Razor ſet,
    it wounds with treach'rous Lies.

3, 4 Thy

3,4 Thy Thoughts are more on Ill than Good,
    on Lies than Truth, employ'd;
  Thy Tongue delights in Words, by which
    the Guiltless are destroy'd.
5 God shall for ever blast thy Hopes,
    and snatch thee soon away;
  Nor in thy Dwelling-place permit,
    nor in the World, to stay.
6 The Just, with pious Fear, shall see
    the Downfall of thy Pride,
  And at thy sudden Ruin laugh,
    and thus thy Fall deride:
7 " See there the Man that haughty was,
  " who proudly God defy'd,
  " Who trusted in his Wealth, and still
  " on wicked Arts rely'd."
8 But I am like those Olive Plants
    that shade God's Temple round
  And hope with His indulgent Grace
    to be for ever crown'd.
9 So shall my Soul with Praise, O God,
    extol thy wond'rous Love;
  And on thy Name with Patience wait,
    for this thy Saints approve.

PSALM LIII.

1 THE wicked Fools must, sure, suppose,
    that God is but a Name:
  This gross Mistake their Practice shows,
    since Virtue all disclaim.
2 The Lord look'd down from Heav'n's high Tow'rs
    the Sons of Men to view,
  To see if any own'd His Pow'r,
    or Truth or Justice knew.
3 But all, He saw, were backward gone,
    degen'rate grown, and base;
  None for Religion car'd, not one
    of all the sinful Race.
4 But are those Workers of Deceit
    so dull and senseless grown,
  That they, like Bread, my People eat,
    and God's just Pow'r disown?

5 Their causeless Fears shall strangely grow;
    and they, despis'd of God,
Shall soon be foil'd: His Hand shall throw
    their shatter'd Bones abroad.
6 Would He his saving Pow'r employ
    to break our servile Band,
Loud Shouts of universal Joy
    should echo thro' the Land.

PSALM LIV.

1, 2 LORD, save me, for thy glorious Name;
    and in thy Strength appear
To judge my Cause; accept my Pray'r
    and to my Words give Ear.
3 Mere Strangers, whom I never wrong'd,
    to ruin me design'd;
And cruel Men, that fear no God,
    against my Soul combin'd.
4, 5 But God takes Part with all my Friends;
    and He's the surest Guard:
The God of Truth shall give my Foes
    their Falshood's just Reward;
6 While I my grateful Off'rings bring,
    and sacrifice with Joy,
And in his Praise my Time to come
    delightfully employ.
7 From dreadful Danger and Distress
    the Lord hath set me free:
Thro' Him shall I of all my Foes
    the just Destruction see.

PSALM LV.

1 GIVE Ear, thou Judge of all the Earth,
    and listen when I pray;
Nor from thy humble Suppliant turn
    thy glorious Face away.
2 Attend to this my sad Complaint,
    and hear my grievous Moans,
Whilst I my mournful Case declare
    with artless Sighs and Groans.
3 Hark, how the Foe insults aloud!
    how fierce Oppressors rage!

Whose sland'rous Tongues with wrathful Hate
  against my Fame engage.
4, 5 My Heart is rack'd with Pain; my Soul
  with deadly Frights distress'd,
With Fear and Trembling compass'd round,
  with Horror quite oppress'd.
6 How often wish'd I then, that I
  the Dove's swift Wings could get;
That I might take my speedy Flight,
  and seek a safe Retreat.
7, 8 Then would I wander far from hence,
  and in wild Deserts stray,
Till all this furious Storm were spent,
  this Tempest past away.

PART II.

9 Destroy, O Lord, their ill Designs,
  their Counsels soon divide;
For, thro' the City my griev'd Eyes
  have Strife and Rapine spy'd.
10 By Day and Night, on ev'ry Wall,
  they walk their constant Round,
And, in the Midst of all her Strength,
  are Grief and Mischief found.
11 Whoe'er thro' ev'ry Part shall roam
  will fresh Disorders meet:
Deceit and Guile their constant Post
  maintain in ev'ry Street.
12 For, 'twas not any open Foe
  that false Reflections made;
For, then I could with Ease have borne
  the bitter Things he said:
'Twas none who Hatred had profess'd,
  that did against me rise;
For, then I had withdrawn myself
  From his malicious Eyes:
13, 14 But 'twas e'en thou, my Guide, my Friend,
  whom tend'rest Love did join;
Whose sweet Advice I valu'd most,
  whose Pray'rs were mix'd with mine.
15 Sure Vengeance equal to their Crimes
  such Traitors must surprise;

And

And sudden Death requite those Ills
   they wickedly devise.
16, 17 But I will call on God, who still
   shall in my Aid appear :
At Morn, and Noon, and Night I'll pray,
   and He my Voice shall hear.

PART III.

18 God has releas'd my Soul from those
   that did with me contend,
And made a num'rous Host of Friends
   my righteous Cause defend.
19 For He, who was my Help of old,
   shall now his Suppliant hear ;
And punish them, whose prosp'rous State
   makes them no God to fear.
20 Whom can I trust, if faithless Men
   perfidiously devise
To ruin me, their peaceful Friend,
   and break the strongest Ties ?
21 Tho' soft and melting are their Words,
   their Hearts with War abound :
Their Speeches are more smooth than Oil,
   and yet like Swords they wound.
22 Do thou, my Soul, on God depend,
   and He shall thee sustain :
He aids the Just, whom to supplant
   the Wicked strive in vain.
23 My Foes, that trade in Lies and Blood,
   shall all untimely die ;
Whilst I for Health and Length of Days
   on Thee, my God, rely.

PSALM LVI.

1 DO Thou, O God, in Mercy help,
      for Man my Life pursues :
To crush me with repeated Wrongs
   he daily Strife renews.
2 Continually my spiteful Foes
   to ruin me combine :
Thou see'st who sitt'st, enthron'd on high,
   what mighty Numbers join.

PSALM lvi.

3 But, tho' sometimes surpriz'd by Fear
    (on Danger's first Alarm),
  Yet still for Succour I depend
    on thy Almighty Arm.
4 God's faithful Promise I shall praise,
    on which I now rely:
  In God I trust, and, trusting Him,
    the Arm of Flesh defy.
5 They wrest my Words, and make them speak
    a Sense they never meant:
  Their Thoughts are all, with restless Spite,
    on my Destruction bent.
6 In close Assemblies they combine,
    and wicked Projects lay:
  They watch my Steps, and lie in wait
    to make my Soul their Prey.
7 Shall such Injustice still escape?
    O righteous God, arise:
  Let thy just Wrath (too long provok'd)
    this impious Race chastise.
8 Thou numb'rest all my wand'ring Steps,
    since first compell'd to flee:
  My very Tears are treasur'd up
    and register'd by Thee.
9 When, therefore, I invoke thy Aid,
    my Foes shall be o'erthrown;
  For, I am well assur'd that God
    my righteous Cause will own.
10, 11 I'll trust God's Word, and so despise
    the Force that Man can raise:
12 To Thee, O God, my Vows are due;
    to Thee I'll render Praise:
13 Thou hast retriev'd my Soul from Death;
    and Thou wilt still secure
  The Life Thou hast so oft preserv'd,
    and make my Footsteps sure:
  That, thus protected by thy Pow'r,
    I may this Light enjoy;
  And in the Service of my God
    my lengthen'd Days employ.

PSALM LVII.

1 THY Mercy, Lord, to me extend:
  On thy Protection I depend;
  And to thy Wings for Shelter haste,
  Till this outrageous Storm is past.
2 To thy Tribunal, Lord, I fly,
  Thou Sov'reign Judge, and God most High,
  Who Wonders hast for me begun,
  And wilt not leave thy Work undone.
3 From Heav'n protect me by thy Arm,
  And shame all those who seek my Harm:
  To my Relief thy Mercy send,
  And Truth, on which my Hopes depend.
4 For I with savage Men converse,
  Like hungry Lions wild and fierce;
  With Men whose Teeth are Spears, their Words
  Invenom'd Darts and two-edg'd Swords.
5 Be Thou, O God, exalted high;
  And, as thy Glory fills the Sky,
  So let it be on Earth display'd;
  Till Thou art here, as there, obey'd.
6 To take me they their Net prepar'd,
  And had almost my Soul ensnar'd;
  But fell themselves, by just Decree,
  Into the Pit they made for me.
7 O God, my Heart is fix'd, 'tis bent,
  Its thankful Tribute to present;
  And, with my Heart, my Voice I'll raise
  To Thee, my God, in Songs of Praise.
8 Awake, my Glory; Harp and Lute,
  No longer let your Strings be mute;
  And I, my tuneful Part to take,
  Will with the early Dawn awake:
9 Thy Praises, Lord, I will resound
  To all the list'ning Nations round:
10 Thy Mercy highest Heav'n transcends;
  Thy Truth beyond the Clouds extends.
11 Be Thou, O God, exalted high;
  And, as thy Glory fills the Sky,
  So let it be on Earth display'd,
  Till Thou art here, as there, obey'd.

PSALM LVIII.

1 SPEAK, O ye Judges of the Earth,
　if juſt your Sentence be;
Or muſt not Innocence appeal
　to Heav'n from your Decree?

2 Your wicked Hearts and Judgments are
　alike by Malice ſway'd;
Your griping Hands, by weighty Bribes,
　to Violence betray'd.

3 To Virtue Strangers from the Womb,
　their Infant Steps went wrong:
They prattled Slander, and in Lies
　employ'd their liſping Tongue.

4 No Serpent of parch'd Afric's Breed
　does ranker Poiſon bear:
The drowſy Adder will as ſoon
　unlock his ſullen Ear.

5 Unmov'd by good Advice, and deaf
　as Adders, they remain;
From whom the ſkilful Charmer's Voice
　can no attention gain.

6 Defeat, O God, their threat'ning Rage,
　And timely break their Pow'r:
Diſarm theſe growling Lions' Jaws,
　e'er practis'd to devour.

7 Let now their Inſolence, at Height,
　like ebbing Tides be ſpent;
Their ſhiver'd Darts deceive their Aim,
　when they their Bow have bent.

8 Like Snails let them diſſolve to Slime;
　like haſty Births become;
Unworthy to behold the Sun,
　and dead within the Womb.

9 Ere Thorns can make the Fleſh-pots boil,
　tempeſtuous Wrath ſhall come
From God, and ſnatch them hence, alive,
　to their eternal Doom.

10 The Righteous ſhall rejoice to ſee
　their Crimes ſuch Vengeance meet;
And Saints in Perſecutors' Blood
　ſhall dip their harmleſs Feet.

11 Transgressors then with Grief shall see
    just Men Rewards obtain;
And own a God, whose Justice will
    the guilty Earth arraign.

PSALM LIX.

1 DELIVER me, O Lord, my God;
    from all my spiteful Foes;
In my Defence oppose thy Pow'r
    to theirs who me oppose.

2 Preserve me from a wicked Race;
    who make a Trade of Ill;
Protect me from remorseless Men,
    who seek my Blood to spill.

3 They lie in Wait, and mighty Pow'rs
    against my Life combine;
Implacable; yet, Lord, Thou know'st;
    for no Offence of mine.

4 In Haste they run about, and watch
    my guiltless Life to take:
Look down, O Lord, on my Distress,
    and to my Help awake.

5 Thou, Lord of Hosts, and Israel's God,
    their Heathen Rage suppress;
Relentless Vengeance take on those
    who stubbornly transgress.

6 At Ev'ning to beset my House
    like growling Dogs they meet;
While others through the City range,
    and ransack ev'ry Street.

7 Their Throats envenom'd Slander breathe;
    their Tongues are sharpen'd Swords:
    " Who hears, (say they) or hearing dares
    " reprove our lawless Words?"

8 But from thy Throne Thou shalt, O Lord,
    their baffled Plots deride:
And soon to Scorn and Shame expose
    their boasted Heathen Pride:

9 On Thee I wait; 'tis on thy Strength
    for Succour I depend:
'Tis Thou, O God, art my Defence,
    who only canst defend.

F   10 Thy

10 Thy Mercy, Lord, which haſt ſo oft
from Danger ſet me free,
Shall crown my Wiſhes, and ſubdue
my haughty Foes to me.
11 Deſtroy them not, O Lord, at once;
reſtrain thy vengeful Blow;
Left we, ungratefully, too ſoon
forget their Overthrow.
Diſperſe them thro' the Nations round
by thy avenging Pow'r:
Do Thou bring down their haughty Pride,
O Lord, our Shield and Tow'r.
12 Now, in the Height of all their Hopes,
their Arrogance chaſtiſe;
Whoſe Tongues have ſinn'd without Reſtraint,
and Curſes join'd with Lies.
13 Nor ſhalt Thou, whilſt their Race endures,
thine Anger, Lord, ſuppreſs;
That diſtant Lands, by their juſt Doom,
may *Iſrael's* God confeſs.
14 At Ev'ning let them ſtill perſiſt
like growling Dogs to meet:
Still wander all the City round,
and traverſe ev'ry Street.
15 Then, as for Malice now they do,
for Hunger let them ſtray;
And yell their vain Complaints aloud,
defeated of their Prey.
16 Whilſt early I thy Mercy ſing,
thy wondrous Pow'r confeſs;
For Thou haſt been my ſure Defence,
my Refuge in Diſtreſs.
17 To Thee, with never-ceaſing Praiſe,
O God, my Strength, I'll ſing;
Thou art my God, the Rock from whence
my Health and Safety ſpring.

PSALM LX.

1 O GOD, who haſt our Troops diſpers'd,
Forſaking thoſe who left Thee firſt;
As we thy juſt Diſpleaſure mourn,
To us, in Mercy, Lord, return.

2 Our Strength, that firm as Earth did stand,
 Is rent by thy avenging Hand:
 O! heal the Breaches Thou hast made:
 We shake, we fall, without thy Aid!
3 Our Folly's sad Effects we feel;
 For, drunk with Discord's Cup, we reel.
4 But now, for them who Thee rever'd,
 Thou hast thy Truth's bright Banner rear'd.
5 Let thy Right-hand thy Saints protect:
 Lord, hear the Pray'rs that we direct.
6 The Holy God has spoke; and I,
 O'erjoy'd, on his firm Word rely.
 To thee in Portions I'll divide
 Fair *Sichem's* Soil, *Samaria's* Pride:
 To *Sichem*, *Succoth* next I'll join,
 And measure out her Vale by Line.
7 *Manasseh*, *Gilead*, both subscribe
 To my Commands, with *Ephraim's* Tribe;
 Ephraim by Arms supports my Cause,
 And *Judah* by religious Laws.
8 *Moab* my Slave and Drudge shall be,
 Nor *Edom* from my Yoke get free;
 Proud *Palestine's* imperious State
 Shall humbly on our Triumph wait.
9 But who shall quell those mighty Pow'rs,
 And clear my Way to *Edom's* Tow'rs?
 Or through her guarded Frontiers tread
 The Path that does to Conquest lead?
10 Ev'n Thou, O God, who hast dispers'd
 Our Troops (for we forsook Thee first),
 Those whom Thou didst in Wrath forsake,
 Aton'd, Thou wilt victorious make.
11 Do Thou our fainting Cause sustain;
 For human Succours are but vain.
12 Fresh Strength and Courage God bestows:
 'Tis He treads down our proudest Foes.

PSALM LXI.

1 LORD, hear my Cry, regard my Pray'r,
  which I, oppress'd with Grief,
2 From Earth's remotest Parts address
  to Thee for kind Relief.

  O lodge me safe, beyond the Reach
   of persecuting Pow'r;
3 Thou, who so oft from spiteful Foes
   hast been my shelt'ring Tow'r.
4 So shall I in thy sacred Courts
   secure from Danger lie:
 Beneath the Covert of thy Wings
   all future Storms defy.
5 In Sign my Vows are heard, once more
   I o'er thy Chosen reign!
6 O! bless with long and prosp'rous Life
   the King Thou didst ordain:
7 Confirm his Throne, and make his Reign
   accepted in thy Sight:
 And let thy Truth and Mercy both
   in his Defence unite.
8 So shall I ever sing thy Praise,
   thy Name for ever bless;
 Devote my prosp'rous Days to pay
   the Vows of my Distress.

PSALM LXII.

1,2 MY Soul for Help on God relies;
   from Him alone my Safety flows:
 My Rock, my Health, that Strength supplies,
   to bear the Shock of all my Foes.
3 How long will ye contrive my Fall,
   which will but hasten on your own?
 You'll totter like a bending Wall,
   or Fence of uncemented Stone.
4 To make my envy'd Honours less,
   they strive with Lies, their chief Delight;
 For they, tho' with their Mouths they bless,
   in private curse with inward Spite.
5,6 But thou, my Soul, on God rely;
   on Him alone thy Trust repose:
 My Rock and Health will Strength supply
   to bear the Shock of all my Foes.
7 God does his saving Health dispense,
   and flowing Blessings daily send:
 He is my Fortress and Defence,
   on Him my Soul shall still depend.

PSALM lxii, lxiii.

8 In Him, ye People, always trust;
  before his Throne pour out your Hearts;
For God, the Merciful and Just,
  his timely Aid to us imparts.
9 The Vulgar fickle are and frail;
  the Great diffemble and betray;
And, laid in Truth's impartial Scale,
  the lightest Things will both outweigh.
10 Then trust not in oppreffive Ways;
   by Spoil and Rapine grow not vain;
Nor let your Hearts, if Wealth increafe,
   be fet too much upon your Gain.
11 For God has oft his Will exprefs'd,
   and I this Truth have fully known;
To be of boundlefs Power poffefs'd
   belongs of Right to God alone.
12 Though Mercy is his darling Grace,
   in which He chiefly takes Delight;
Yet will He all the human Race
   according to their Works requite.

PSALM LXIII.

1 O GOD, my gracious God, to Thee
   My morning Prayers fhall offer'd be;
  for Thee my thirfty Soul does pant;
My fainting Flefh implores thy Grace,
Within this dry and barren Place,
  where I refrefhing Waters want.
2 O! to my longing Eyes, once more
That View of glorious Power reftore,
  which thy majeftic Houfe difplays:
3 Becaufe to me thy wondrous Love
Than Life itfelf does dearer prove,
  my Lips fhall always fpeak thy Praife.
4 My Life, while I that Life enjoy,
In bleffing God I will employ;
  with lifted Hands adore his Name;
5 My Soul's Content fhall be as great
As theirs who choiceft Dainties eat,
  while I with Joy his Praife proclaim.
6 When down I lie fweet Sleep to find,
Thou, Lord, art prefent to my Mind;
  and when I wake in Dead of Night;

7 Be-

7 Becaufe Thou ftill doft Succour bring,
   Beneath the Shadow of thy Wing
     I reft with Safety and Delight.
8 My Soul, when Foes would me devour,
   Cleaves faft to Thee, whofe matchlefs Pow'r
     in her Support is daily fhown :
9 But thofe the righteous Lord fhall flay,
   That my Deftruction wifh; and they
     that feek my Life, fhall loofe their own.
10, 11 They by untimely Ends fhall die,
   Their Flefh a Prey to Foxes lie;
     but God fhall fill the King with Joy;
   Who fwears by Thee, fhall ftill rejoice;
   Whilft the falfe Tongue and lying Voice,
     Thou, Lord, fhalt filence and deftroy.

PSALM LXIV.

1 LORD, hear the Voice of my Complaint,
     to my Requeft give Ear;
   Preferve my Life from cruel Foes,
     and free my Soul from Fear.
2 O! hide me with thy tend'reft Care,
     in fome fecure Retreat,
   From Sinners that againft me rife;
     and all their Plots defeat.
3 See how, intent to work my Harm,
     they whet their Tongues like Swords;
   And bend their Bows to fhoot their Darts,
     fharp Lies and bitter Words.
4 Lurking in private, at the Juft
     they take their fecret Aim;
   And fuddenly at him they fhoot,
     quite void of Fear and Shame.
5 To carry on their ill Defigns
     they mutually agree;
   They fpeak of laying private Snares,
     and think that none fhall fee.
6 With utmoft Diligence and Care
     their wicked Plots they lay;
   The deep Defigns of all their Hearts
     are only to betray.

PSALM lxiv, lxv.

7 But God, to Anger juſtly mov'd,
    his dreadful Bow ſhall bend,
And on his flying Arrow's Point
    ſhall ſwift Deſtruction ſend.
8 Thoſe Slanders which their Mouths did vent
    upon themſelves ſhall fall:
Their Crimes diſclos'd ſhall make them be
    deſpis'd and ſhunn'd by all.
9 The World ſhall then God's Power confeſs,
    and Nations trembling ſtand;
Convinc'd that 'tis the mighty Work
    of his avenging Hand.
10 Whilſt righteous Men, by God ſecur'd,
    in Him ſhall gladly truſt;
And all the liſt'ning Earth ſhall hear
    loud Triumphs of the Juſt.

PSALM LXV.

1 FOR Thee, O God, our conſtant Praiſe
    in *Sion* waits, thy choſen Seat:
Our promis'd Altars there we'll raiſe,
    nd all our zealous Vows complete.
2 O Thou, who to my humble Pray'r
    didſt always bend thy liſt'ning Ear,
To Thee ſhall all Mankind repair,
    and at thy gracious Throne appear.
3 Our Sins (tho' numberleſs) in vain
    to ſtop thy flowing Mercy try;
Whilſt thou o'erlook'ſt the guilty Stain,
    and waſheſt out the Crimſon Dye.
4 Bleſt is the Man who, near Thee plac'd,
    within thy ſacred Dwelling lives;
Whilſt we, at humbler Diſtance, taſte
    the vaſt Delights thy Temple gives.
5 By wondrous Acts, O God, moſt juſt,
    have we thy gracious Anſwer found:
In Thee remoteſt Nations truſt,
    and thoſe whom ſtormy Waves ſurround.
6, 7 God, by his Strength, ſets faſt the Hills,
    and does his matchleſs Pow'r engage;
With which the Seas loud Waves he ſtills,
    and angry Crowds' tumultuous Rage.

8 Thou,

8 Thou, Lord, doſt barb'rous Lands diſmay,
 when they thy dreadful Tokens view:
With Joy they ſee the Night and Day
 each other's Track, by Turns, purſue.
9 From out thy unexhauſted Store
 thy Rain relieves the thirſty Ground;
Makes Lands, that barren were before,
 with Corn and uſeful Fruits abound.
10 On riſing Ridges down it pours,
 and every furrow'd Valley fills;
Thou mak'ſt them ſoft with gentle Show'rs,
 in which a bleſt Increaſe diſtils.
11 Thy Goodneſs does the circling Year
 with freſh Returns of Plenty crown;
And where thy glorious Paths appear,
 the fruitful Clouds drop Fatneſs down.
12 They drop on barren Foreſts, chang'd
 by them to Paſtures freſh and green;
The Hills about, in Order rang'd,
 in beauteous Robes of Joy are ſeen.
13 Large Flocks with fleecy Wool adorn
 the cheerful Downs; the Vallies bring
A plenteous Crop of full-ear'd Corn,
 and ſeem for Joy to ſhout and ſing.

PSALM LXVI.

1,2 LET all the Lands with Shouts of Joy
 to God their Voices raiſe;
Sing Pſalms in honour of his Name,
 and ſpread his glorious Praiſe.
3 And let them ſay, How dreadful, Lord,
 in all thy Works, art Thou;
To thy great Pow'r thy ſtubborn Foes
 ſhall all be forc'd to bow.
4 Thro' all the Earth the Nations round
 ſhall Thee their God confeſs,
And, with glad Hymns, their awful Dread
 of thy great Name expreſs.
5 O! come, behold the Works of God,
 and then with me you'll own,
That He to all the Sons of Men
 has wondrous Judgments ſhown.

PSALM lxvi.

6 He made the Sea become dry Land,
   through which our Fathers walk'd;
Whilst to each other of his Might
   with Joy his People talk'd.
7 He, by his Pow'r, for ever rules;
   his Eyes the World survey:
Let no presumptuous Man rebel
   against his sov'reign Sway.

PART II.

8, 9 O! all ye Nations, bless our God,
   and loudly speak his Praise;
Who keeps our Soul alive, and still
   confirms our stedfast Ways.
10 For thou hast try'd us, Lord, as Fire
   does try the precious Ore:
11 Thou brought'st us into Streights, where we
   oppressing Burdens bore.
12 Insulting Foes did us, their Slaves,
   through Fire and Water chace;
But yet at last thou brought'st us forth
   into a wealthy Place.
13 Burnt Off'rings to thy House I'll bring,
   and there my Vows I'll pay;
14 Which I with solemn Zeal did make
   in Trouble's dismal Day.
15 Then shall the richest Incense smoke,
   the fattest Rams shall fall;
The choicest Goats from out the Fold,
   and Bullocks from the Stall.
16 O! come, all ye that fear the Lord;
   attend with heedful Care,
Whilst I, what God for me has done,
   with grateful Joy declare.
17, 18 As I before his Aid implor'd,
   so now I praise his Name,
Who, if my Heart had harbour'd Sin,
   would all my Pray'rs disclaim.
19 But God to me, whene'er I cry'd,
   his gracious Ear did bend;
And to the Voice of my Request,
   with constant Love attend.

20 Then

20 Then bless'd for ever be my God,
   who never, when I pray,
With-holds his Mercy from my Soul,
   nor turns his Face away.

PSALM LXVII.

1 TO bless thy chosen Race,
   in Mercy, Lord, incline,
And cause the Brightness of thy Face
   on all thy Saints to shine.
2 That so thy wondrous Way
   may thro' the World be known;
While distant Lands their Tribute pay,
   and thy Salvation own.
3 Let diff'ring Nations join
   to celebrate thy Fame;
Let all the World, O Lord, combine
   to praise thy glorious Name.
4 O let them shout and sing,
   dissolv'd in pious Mirth;
For Thou, the righteous Judge and King,
   shalt govern all the Earth.
5 Let diff'ring Nations join
   to celebrate thy Fame;
Let all the World, O Lord, combine
   to praise thy glorious Name.
6 Then shall the teeming Ground
   a large Increase disclose;
And we with Plenty shall be crown'd,
   which God, our God, bestows.
7 Then God upon our Land
   shall constant Blessings show'r;
And all the World in Awe shall stand
   of his resistless Pow'r.

PSALM LXVIII.

1 LET God, the God of Battle, rise,
   and scatter his presumptuous Foes;
Let shameful Rout their Host surprise,
   who spitefully his Pow'r oppose.
2 As Smoke in Tempest's Rage is lost,
   or Wax into the Furnace cast,

PSALM lxviii.

So let their facrilegious Hoſt
 before his wrathful Preſence waſte.
3 But let the Servants of his Will
 his Favour's gentle Beams enjoy:
 Their upright Hearts let Gladneſs fill,
 and chearful Songs their Tongues employ.
4 To him your Voice in Anthems raiſe:
 JEHOVAH's awful Name he bears:
 In Him rejoice, extol his Praiſe,
 who rides upon high-rolling Spheres.
5 Him, from his Empire of the Skies,
 to this low World Compaſſion draws,
 The Orphan's Claim to patronize,
 and judge the injur'd Widow's Cauſe.
6 'Tis God, who from a foreign Soil
 reſtores poor Exiles to their Home;
 Makes Captives free, and fruitleſs Toil
 their proud Oppreſſors righteous Doom.
7 'Twas ſo of old, when Thou didſt lead
 in Perſon, Lord, our Armies forth;
 Strange Terrors through the Deſert ſpread,
 Convulſions ſhook th' aſtoniſh'd Earth.
8 The breaking Clouds did Rain diſtil,
 and Heav'n's high Arches ſhook with Fear:
 How then ſhall *Sinai's* humble Hill
 of *Iſrael's* God the Preſence bear?
9 Thy Hand, at famiſh'd Earth's Complaint,
 reliev'd her from celeſtial Stores,
 And when thy Heritage was faint,
 aſſwag'd the Drought with plenteous Show'rs.
10 Where Savages had rang'd before,
 at Eaſe Thou mad'ſt our Tribes reſide;
 And, in the Deſert, for the Poor
 thy gen'rous Bounty did provide.

PART II.

11 Thou gav'ſt the Word, we ſally'd forth,
 and in that pow'rful Word o'ercame:
 While Virgin Troops, with Songs of Mirth,
 in State our Conqueſt did proclaim.
12 Vaſt Armies, by ſuch Gen'rals led,
 as yet had ne'er receiv'd a Foil,

Forſook

PSALM lxviii.

Forsook their Camp with sudden Dread,
  and to our Women left the Spoil.
13 Though *Egypt's* Drudges you have been,
  your Army's Wings shall shine as bright
As Doves in golden Sunshine seen,
  or silver'd o'er with paler Light.
14 'Twas so, when God's Almighty Hand
  o'er scatter'd Kings the Conquest won:
Our Troops drawn up on *Jordan's* Strand,
  high *Salmon's* glittering Snow outshone.
15 From thence to *Jordan's* farther Coast,
  and *Bashan's* Hill, we did advance:
No more her Height shall *Bashan* boast,
  but that she's God's Inheritance.
16 But wherefore (tho' the Honour's great)
  should this, O Mountain! swell your Pride?
For *Sion* is his chosen Seat,
  where He for ever will reside.
17 His Chariots numberless; his Powers
  are heavenly Hosts that wait his Will;
His Presence now fills *Sion's* Tow'rs,
  as once it honour'd *Sinai's* Hill.
18 Ascending high, in Triumph Thou
  Captivity hast Captive led;
And on thy People didst bestow
  the Spoil of Armies, once their Dread.
Ev'n Rebels shall partake thy Grace,
  and humble Proselytes repair
To worship at thy Dwelling-place,
  and all the World pay Homage there.
19 For Benefits each Day bestow'd
  be daily his great Name ador'd!
20 Who is our Saviour and our God,
  of Life and Death the Sov'reign Lord.
21 But Justice for his harden'd Foes
  proportion'd Vengeance has decreed,
To wound the hoary Head of those
  who in presumptuous Crimes proceed.
22 The Lord has thus in Thunder spoke;
  " As I subdued proud *Bashan's* King,
" Once more I'll break my People's Yoke,
" and from the Deep my Servants bring.

23 " Their

PSALM lxviii.

23 " Their Feet shall with a Crimson Flood
" of slaughter'd Foes be cover'd o'er:
" Nor Earth receive such impious Blood
" but leave for Dogs th' unhallow'd Gore."

PART III.

24 When marching to thy blest Abode,
    the wond'ring Multitude survey'd
The pompous State of Thee, our God,
    in Robes of Majesty array'd;
25 Sweet-singing Levites led the Van;
    loud Instruments brought up the Rear;
Between both Troops a Virgin Train
    with Voice and Timbrel charm'd the Ear;
26 This was the Burthen of their Song:
    " In full Assemblies bless the Lord:
" And who to *Israel's* Tribes belong,
    " the God of *Israel's* Praise record."
27 Not little *Benjamin* alone
    from neighb'ring Bounds did there attend,
Nor only *Judah's* nearer Throne
    her Counsellors in State did send;
But *Zebulon's* remoter Seat,
    and *Naphtali's* more distant Coast,
(The grand Procession to complete)
    sent up their Tribes, a princely Host.
28 Thus God to Strength and Union brought
    our Tribes, at Strife till that blest Hour.
This Work, which Thou, O God, hast wrought,
    confirm with fresh Recruits of Pow'r.
29 To visit *Salem*, Lord, descend,
    and *Sion*, thy terrestrial Throne;
Where Kings with Presents shall attend,
    and Thee with offer'd Crowns atone.
30 Break down the Spearmen's Ranks, who threat
    like pamper'd Herds of Savage Might;
Their silver-armour'd Chiefs defeat,
    who in destructive War delight.
31 *Egypt* shall then to God stretch forth
    her Hands, and *Afric* Homage bring;
32 The scatter'd Kingdoms of the Earth
    their common Sovereign's Praises sing.

33 Who, mounted on the loftiest Sphere
   of antient Heav'n, sublimely rides;
   From whence his dreadful Voice we hear,
   like that of warring Winds and Tides.
34 Ascribe the Pow'r to God most High:
   of humble *Israel* he takes Care;
   Whose Strength from out the dusky Sky
   darts shining Terrors through the Air.
35 How dreadful are the sacred Courts,
   where God has fix'd his earthly Throne!
   His Strength his feeble Saints supports:
   to God give Praise, and Him alone.

PSALM LXIX.

1 SAVE me, O God, from Waves that roll,
   And press to overwhelm my Soul.
2 With painful Steps in Mire I tread,
   And Deluges o'erflow my Head.
3 With restless Cries my Spirits faint;
   My Voice is hoarse with long Complaint;
   My Sight decays with tedious Pain,
   Whilst for my God I wait in vain.
4 My Hairs, tho' num'rous, are but few
   Compar'd with Foes that me pursue
   With groundless Hate, grown now of Might
   To execute their lawless Spite:
   They force me guiltless to resign
   As Rapine, what by Right was mine.
5 Thou, Lord, my Innocence dost see,
   Nor are my Sins conceal'd from Thee.
6 Lord God of Hosts, take timely Care,
   Lest, for my Sake, thy Saints despair;
7 Since I have suffer'd for thy Name
   Reproach, and hid my Face in Shame:
8 A Stranger to my Country grown,
   Nor to my dearest Kindred known;
   A Foreigner, expos'd to Scorn
   By Brethren of my Mother born.
9 For Zeal to thy lov'd House and Name
   Consumes me like devouring Flame;
   Concern'd at their Affronts to Thee,
   More than at Slanders cast on me.

PSALM lxix.

10 My very Tears and Abstinence
   They construe in a spiteful Sense:
11 When cloath'd in Sackcloth for their Sake,
   They me their common Proverb make.
12 Their Judges make my Wrongs their Jest,
   Those Wrongs they ought to have redress'd.
   How should I then expect to be
   From Libels of lewd Drunkards free?
13 But, Lord, to Thee I will repair
   For Help, with humble timely Pray'r:
   Relieve me from thy Mercy's Store:
   Display thy Truth's preserving Pow'r.
14 From threat'ning Dangers me relieve;
   And from the Mire my Feet retrieve;
   From spiteful Foes in Safety keep,
   And snatch me from the raging Deep.
15 Controul the Deluge ere it spread,
   And roll its Waves above my Head;
   Nor deep Destruction's yawning Pit
   To close her Jaws on me permit.
16 Lord, hear the humble Prayer I make,
   For thy transcending Goodness' Sake;
   Relieve thy Supplicant once more
   From thy abounding Mercy's Store,
17 Nor from thy Servant hide thy Face:
   Make haste; for desp'rate is my Case:
18 Thy timely Succour interpose,
   And shield me from remorseless Foes.
19 Thou know'st what Infamy and Scorn
   I from my Enemies have borne;
   Nor can their close dissembled Spite,
   Or darkest Plots, escape thy Sight.
20 Reproach and Grief have broke my Heart:
   I look'd for some to take my Part,
   To pity, or relieve my Pain:
   But look'd, alas! for both in vain.
21 With Hunger pin'd, for Food I call;
   Instead of Food they give me Gall:
   And when with Thirst my Spirits sink,
   They gave me Vinegar to drink.
22 Their Table, therefore, to their Health
   Shall prove a Snare, a Trap their Wealth:

23 Perpetual

23 Perpetual Darkness seize their Eyes,
   And sudden Blasts their Hopes surprize.
24 On them thou shalt thy Fury pour;
   Till thy fierce Wrath their Race devour;
25 And make their House a dismal Cell,
   Where none will e'er vouchsafe to dwell.
26 For new Afflictions they procur'd
   For him who had thy Stripes endur'd;
   And made the Wounds thy Scourge had torn,
   To bleed afresh, with sharper Scorn.
27 Sin shall to Sin their Steps betray,
   Till they to Truth have lost the Way.
28 From Life Thou shalt exclude their Soul,
   Nor with the Just their Names enrol.
29 But me, howe'er distress'd and poor,
   Thy strong Salvation shall restore.
30 Thy Pow'r with Songs I'll then proclaim,
   And celebrate with Thanks thy Name.
31 Our God shall this more highly prize
   Than Herds and Flocks in Sacrifice.
32 Which humble Saints with Joy shall see,
   And hope for like Redress with me.
33 For God regards the Poor's Complaint;
   Sets Pris'ners free from close Restraint.
34 Let Heav'n, Earth, Sea, their Voices raise,
   And all the World resound his Praise.
35 For God will Sion's Walls erect;
   Fair Judah's Cities He'll protect;
   Till all her scatter'd Sons repair
   To undisturb'd Possession there.
36 This Blessing they shall, at their Death,
   To their religious Heirs bequeath;
   And they to endless Ages more,
   Of such as his blest Name adore.

PSALM LXX.

1 O LORD, to my Relief draw near;
   for never was more pressing Need:
   For my Deliv'rance, Lord, appear,
   and add to that Deliv'rance Speed.
2 Confusion on their Heads return,
   who to destroy my Soul combine:

Let

PSALM lxx, lxxi.

Let them, defeated, blush and mourn,
  ensnar'd in their own vile Design.
3 Their Doom let Desolation be;
  with Shame their Malice be repaid,
Who mock'd my Confidence in Thee,
  and Sport of my Affliction made.
4 While those, who humbly seek thy Face,
  to joyful Triumphs shall be rais'd;
And all, who prize thy saving Grace,
  with me shall sing, The Lord be prais'd.
5 Thus wretched tho' I am and poor,
  the mighty Lord of me takes Care;
Thou, God, who only canst restore,
  to my Relief with Speed repair.

PSALM LXXI.

1, 2 IN Thee I put my stedfast Trust;
  defend me, Lord, from Shame;
Incline thine Ear, and save my Soul;
  for righteous is thy Name.
3 Be Thou my strong Abiding Place,
  to which I may resort;
'Tis thy Decree that keeps me safe;
  Thou art my Rock and Fort.
4, 5 From cruel and ungodly Men
  protect and set me free!
For, from my earliest Youth till now,
  my Hope has been in Thee.
6 Thy constant Care did safely guard
  my tender Infant Days;
Thou took'st me from my Mother's Womb,
  to sing thy constant Praise.
7, 8 While some on me with Wonder gaze,
  thy Hand supports me still;
Thy Honour, therefore, and thy Praise,
  my Mouth shall always fill.
9 Reject not then thy Servant, Lord,
  when I with Age decay;
Forsake me not, when, worn with Years,
  my Vigour fades away.
10 My Foes against my Fame and me
  with crafty Malice speak;

G Against

       Against my Soul they lay their Snares,
         and mutual Counsel take.
11 "His God, say they, forsakes him now,
    "on whom he did rely:
    "Pursue and take Him, whilst no Hope
    "of timely Aid is nigh."
12 But Thou, my God, withdraw not far;
    for speedy Help I call:
13 To Shame and Ruin bring my Foes,
    that seek to work my Fall.
14 But as for me, my stedfast Hope
    shall on thy Pow'r depend;
   And I in grateful Songs of Praise
    my Time to come will spend.

PART II.

15 Thy righteous Acts, and saving Health,
    my Mouth shall still declare;
   Unable yet to count them all,
    tho' summ'd with utmost Care.
16 While God vouchsafes me his Support,
    I'll in his Strength go on:
   All other Righteousness disclaim,
    and mention his alone.
17 Thou, Lord, hast taught me from my Youth
    to praise thy glorious Name:
   And ever since thy wondrous Works
    have been my constant Theme.
18 Then now forsake me not, when I
    am grey and feeble grown;
   Till I to these, and future Times,
    thy Strength and Pow'r have shown:
19 How high thy Justice soars, O God!
    how great and wondrous are
   The mighty Works which Thou hast done!
    who may with Thee compare?
20 Me, whom thy Hand has sorely press'd,
    thy Grace shall yet relieve;
   And, from the lowest Depth of Woe,
    with tender Care retrieve.
21 Through Thee, my Time to come shall be
    with Pow'r and Greatness crown'd;

PSALM lxxi, lxxii.

And me, who dismal Years have pass'd,
   thy Comforts shall surround.
22 Therefore with Psaltery and Harp,
   thy Truth, O Lord, I'll praise;
To Thee, the God of *Jacob's* Race,
   my Voice in Anthems raise.
23 Then Joy shall fill my Mouth, and Songs
   employ my chearful Voice;
My grateful Soul, by Thee redeem'd,
   shall in thy Strength rejoice.
24 My Tongue thy just and righteous Acts
   shall all the Day proclaim;
Because Thou didst confound my Foes,
   and brought'st them all to Shame.

PSALM LXXII.

1 LORD, let thy just Decrees the King
      in all his Ways direct;
And let his Son, throughout his Reign,
   thy righteous Laws respect.
2 So shall he still thy People judge
   with pure and upright Mind;
Whilst all the helpless Poor shall him
   their just Protector find.
3 Then Hills and Mountains shall bring forth
   the happy Fruits of Peace;
Which all the Land shall own to be
   the Work of Righteousness:
4 Whilst he the poor and needy Race
   shall rule with gentle Sway,
And from their humble Necks shall take
   oppressive Yokes away.
5 In ev'ry Heart thy awful Fear
   shall then be rooted fast;
As long as Sun and Moon endure,
   or Time itself shall last.
6 He shall descend like Rain that cheers
   the Meadows' second Birth;
Or like warm Show'rs, whose gentle Drops
   refresh the thirsty Earth.
7 In his blest Days the Just and Good
   shall be with Favour crown'd;

PSALM lxxii.

The happy Land shall ev'ry where
  with endless Peace abound.
8 His uncontrol'd Dominion shall
  from Sea to Sea extend;
Begin at proud Euphrates' Streams,
  at Nature's Limits end.
9 To him the Savage Nations round
  shall bow their servile Heads:
His vanquish'd Foes shall lick the Dust,
  where he his Conquests spreads.
10 The Kings of *Tarshish*, and the Isles,
  shall costly Presents bring;
From spicy *Sheba* Gifts shall come,
  and wealthy *Saba's* King.
11 To him shall ev'ry King on Earth
  his humble Homage pay,
And diff'ring Nations gladly join
  to own his righteous Sway.
12 For he shall set the Needy free;
  when they for Succour cry;
Shall save the Helpless and the Poor,
  and all their Wants supply.

PART II.

13 His Providence for needy Souls
  shall due Supplies prepare;
And over their defenceless Lives
  shall watch with tender Care.
14 He shall preserve and keep their Souls
  from Fraud and Rapine free;
And, in his Sight, their guiltless Blood
  of mighty Price shall be.
15 Therefore shall God his Life and Reign
  to many Years extend;
Whilst Eastern Princes Tribute pay,
  and golden Presents send.
For him shall constant Prayers be made
  thro' all his prosp'rous Days;
His just Dominion shall afford
  a lasting Theme of Praise.
16 Of useful Grain, through all the Land,
  great Plenty shall appear;

A Handful sown on Mountain Tops
   a mighty Crop shall bear.
Its Fruits, like Cedars shook by Winds,
   a rattling Noise shall yield:
The City too shall thrive, and vie
   for Plenty with the Field.
17 The Mem'ry of his glorious Name
   thro' endless Years shall run;
His spotless Fame shall shine as bright
   and lasting as the Sun.
In him the Nations of the World
   shall be completely bless'd,
And his unbounded Happiness
   by ev'ry Tongue confess'd.
18 Then bless'd be God, the mighty Lord,
   the God whom *Israel* fears;
Who only wondrous in his Works,
   beyond Compare, appears.
19 Let Earth be with his Glory fill'd;
   for ever bless his Name;
Whilst to his Praise the list'ning World
   their glad Assent proclaim.

PSALM LXXIII.

1 AT length, by certain Proofs, 'tis plain
     that God will to his Saints be kind;
That all, whose Hearts are pure and clean,
   shall his protecting Favour find.
2, 3 Till this sustaining Truth I knew,
   my staggering Feet had almost fail'd;
I griev'd the Sinners' Wealth to view,
   and envy'd when the Fools prevail'd.
4, 5 They to the Grave in Peace descend,
   and, whilst they live, are hale and strong;
No Plagues or Troubles them offend,
   which oft to other Men belong.
6, 7 With Pride, as with a Chain, they're held,
   and Rapine seems their Robe of State:
Their Eyes stand out, with Fatness swell'd;
   they grow, beyond their Wishes, great.
8, 9 With Hearts corrupt, and lofty Talk,
   oppressive Methods they defend;

PSALM lxxiii.

Their Tongue thro' all the Earth does walk,
    their Blasphemies to Heav'n ascend.
10 And yet admiring Crouds are found,
    who servile Visits duly make;
Because with Plenty they abound,
    of which their flatt'ring Slaves partake.
11 Their fond Opinions these pursue,
    till they, with them profanely cry,
" How should the Lord our Actions view?
    " Can He perceive, who dwells so high?"
12 Behold the Wicked! these are they
    who openly their Sins profess;
And yet their Wealth 's increas'd each Day,
    and all their Actions meet Success.
13, 14 " Then have I cleans'd my Heart (said I)
    " and wash'd my Hands from Guilt in vain,
" If all the Day oppress'd I lie,
    " and ev'ry Morning suffer Pain."
15 Thus did I once to speak intend:
    but, if such Things I rashly say,
Thy Children, Lord, I must offend,
    and basely should their Cause betray.

PART II.

16, 17 To fathom this my Thoughts I bent;
    but found the Case too hard for me;
Till to the House of God I went;
    then I their End did plainly see.
18 How high soe'er advanc'd, they all
    on slipp'ry Places loosely stand:
Thence into Ruin headlong fall,
    cast down by thy avenging Hand.
19, 20 How dreadful and how quick their Fate!
    despis'd by Thee, when they're destroy'd:
As waking Men with Scorn do treat
    the Fancies that their Dreams employ'd.
21, 22 Thus was my Heart with Grief oppress'd,
    my Reins were rack'd with endless Pains;
So stupid was I, like a Beast,
    who no reflecting Thought retains.
23, 24 Yet still thy Presence me supply'd,
    and thy Right-hand Assistance gave;

Thou

Thou first shall with thy Counsel guide,
  and then to Glory me receive.
25 Whom then in Heav'n, but Thee alone,
  have I, whose Favour I require?
Throughout the spacious Earth there's none,
  that I, besides Thee, can desire.
26 My trembling Flesh, and aching Heart,
  may often fail to succour me;
But God shall inward Strength impart,
  and my eternal Portion be.
27 For they, that far from Thee remove,
  shall into sudden Ruin fall;
If after other Gods they rove,
  thy Vengeance shall destroy them all.
28 But as for me, 'tis good and just
  that I should still to God repair;
In Him I always put my Trust,
  and will his wondrous Works declare.

PSALM LXXIV.

1 WHY hast Thou cast us off, O God?
   wilt Thou no more return?
Oh! why against thy chosen Flock
  does thy fierce Anger burn?
2 Think on thy antient Purchase, Lord,
  the Land that is thy own,
By Thee redeem'd; and Sion's Mount,
  where once thy Glory shone.
3 Oh! come and view our ruin'd State!
  how long our Troubles last!
See how the Foe, with wicked Rage,
  has laid the Temple waste!
4 Thy Foes blaspheme thy Name: where late
  thy zealous Servants pray'd,
The Heathen there, with haughty Pomp,
  their Banners have display'd.
5, 6 Those curious Carvings, which did once
  advance the Artist's Fame,
With Axe and Hammer they destroy,
  like Works of vulgar Frame.
7 Thy holy Temple they have burn'd;
  and what escap'd the Flame

PSALM lxxiv.

Has been profan'd, and quite defac'd,
tho' facred to thy Name.
8 Thy Worſhip wholly to deſtroy
maliciouſly they aim'd;
And all the ſacred Places burn'd,
where we thy Praiſe proclaim'd.
9 Yet of thy Preſence Thou vouchſaf'dſt
no tender Signs to ſend:
We have no Prophet now, that knows
when this ſad State ſhall end.

PART II.

10 But, Lord, how long wilt Thou permit
th' inſulting Foe to boaſt?
Shall all the Honour of thy Name
for evermore be loſt?
11 Why hold'ſt thou back thy ſtrong Right-hand,
and on thy patient Breaſt,
When Vengeance calls to ſtretch it forth,
ſo calmly lett'ſt it reſt?
12 Thou heretofore, with kingly Pow'r,
in our Defence haſt fought;
For us, throughout the wond'ring World,
haſt great Salvation wrought.
13 'Twas Thou, O God, that didſt the Sea,
by thy own Strength divide:
Thou break'ſt the wat'ry Monſter's Head,
the Waves o'erwhelm'd their Pride.
14 The greateſt, fierceſt of them all,
that ſeem'd the Deep to ſway,
Was by thy Pow'r deſtroy'd, and made
to ſavage Beaſts a Prey.
15 Thou clav'ſt the ſolid Rock, and mad'ſt
the Waters largely flow;
Again, Thou mad'ſt thro' parting Streams
thy wand'ring People go.
16 Thine is the cheerful Day, and thine
the black Return of Night;
Thou haſt prepar'd the glorious Sun,
and ev'ry feebler Light.
17 By Thee the Borders of the Earth
in perfect Order ſtand;

The

The Summer's Warmth, and Winter's Cold,
   attend on thy Command.

PART III.

18 Remember, Lord, how scornful Foes
   have daily urg'd our Shame;
   And how the foolish People have
   blasphem'd thy holy Name.
19 Oh! free thy mourning Turtle-dove,
   by sinful Crowds beset;
   Nor the Assembly of thy Poor
   for evermore forget.
20 Thy ancient Cov'nant, Lord, regard,
   and make thy Promise good;
   For now each Corner of the Land
   is fill'd with Men of Blood.
21 Oh! let not the Opprefs'd return
   with Sorrow cloath'd and Shame;
   But let the Helpless, and the Poor,
   for ever praise thy Name.
22 Arise, O God, in our Behalf;
   thy Cause and our's maintain:
   Remember how insulting Fools
   each Day thy Name profane.
23 Make Thou the Boastings of thy Foes
   for ever, Lord, to cease;
   Whose Insolence, if not chastis'd,
   will more and more increase.

PSALM LXXV.

1 TO Thee, O God, we render Praise,
      to Thee with Thanks repair;
   For, that thy Name to us is nigh,
   thy wondrous Works declare.
2 In *Israel* when my Throne is fixt,
   with me shall Justice reign;
3 The Land with Discord shakes; but I
   the sinking Frame sustain.
4 Deluded Wretches I advis'd
   their Errors to redress;
   And warn'd bold Sinners, that they should
   their swelling Pride suppress.

5 Bear

5 Bear not yourselves so high, as if
 no Pow'r could yours restrain:
 Submit your stubborn Necks, and learn
 to speak with less Disdain.
6 For that Promotion, which to gain,
 your vain Ambition strives,
 From neither East nor West, nor yet
 from Southern Climes, arrives.
7 For God the great Disposer, is,
 and Sov'reign Judge alone,
 Who casts the Proud to Earth, and lifts
 the Humble to a Throne.
8 His Hand holds forth a dreadful Cup;
 with purple Wine 'tis crown'd:
 The deadly Mixture, which his Wrath
 deals out to Nations round.
 Of this his Saints may sometimes taste;
 but wicked Men shall squeeze
 The bitter Dregs, and be condemn'd
 to drink the very Lees.
9 His Prophet, I to all the World
 this Message will relate;
 The Justice then of *Jacob's* God
 my Song shall celebrate.
10 The Wicked's Pride I will reduce,
 their Cruelty disarm;
 Exalt the Just, and seat him high,
 above the Reach of Harm.

PSALM LXXVI.

1 IN *Judah* the Almighty's known,
 (Almighty there, by Wonders shown:)
 his name in *Jacob* does excel:
2 His Sanctuary in *Salem* stands:
 The Majesty that Heav'n commands
 in *Sion* condescends to dwell.
3 He brake the Bow and Arrows there,
 The Shield, the temper'd Sword, and Spear;
 there slain the mighty Army lay.
4 Whence *Sion's* Fame thro' Earth is spread,
 Of greater Glory, greater Dread,
 than Hills, where Robbers lodge their Prey.

5 Their

PSALM lxxvi, lxxvii.

5 Their valiant Chiefs, who came for Spoil,
Themselves met there a shameful Foil:
secureIy down to Sleep they lay,
But wak'd no more; their stoutest Band
Ne'er lifted one resisting Hand
'gainst his that did their Legions slay.
6 When *Jacob's* God began to frown,
Both Horse and Charioteers o'erthrown,
together slept in endless Night.
7 When Thou, whom Heav'n and Earth revere,
Dost once with wrathful Look appear,
what mortal Pow'r can stand thy Sight?
8 Pronounc'd from Heav'n, Earth heard its Doom,
Grew hush'd with Fear, when thou didst come,
9 the Meek with Justice to restore.
10 The Wrath of Man shall yield Thee Praise;
Its last Attempts but serve to raise
the Triumphs of Almighty Pow'r.
11 Vow to the Lord; ye Nations, bring
Vow'd Presents to th' Eternal King:
thus to his Name due Rev'rence pay,
12 Who proudest Potentates can quell,
To earthly Kings more terrible
than to their trembling Subjects they.

PSALM LXXVII.

1 TO God I cry'd, who to my Help
did graciously appear;
2 In Trouble's dismal Day I sought
my God with humble Pray'r.
All Night my fest'ring Wound did run;
no Med'cine gave Relief;
My Soul no Comfort would admit,
my Soul indulg'd her Grief.
3 I thought on God, and Favours past;
but that increas'd my Pain:
I found my Spirit more oppress'd,
the more I did complain.
4 Thro' ev'ry Watch of tedious Night
thou keep'st my Eyes awake;
My Grief is swell'd to that Excess,
I sigh, but cannot speak.

5 I call

5 I call to Mind the Days of old,
　with signal Mercy crown'd :
　Those famous Years of ancient Times
　for Miracles renown'd.
6 By Night I recollect my Songs,
　on former Triumphs made ;
　Then search, consult, and ask my Heart,
　where's now that wondrous Aid ?
7 Has God for ever cast me off ?
　withdrawn his Favour quite ?
8 Are both his Mercy and his Truth
　retir'd to endless Night ?
9 Can his long-practis'd Love forget
　its wonted Aids to bring ?
　Has He in Wrath shut up and seal'd
　his Mercy's healing Spring ;
10 I said, my Weakness hints these Fears ;
　but I'll these fears disband ;
　I'll yet remember the Most High,
　and Years of his Right-hand.
11 I'll call to Mind his Works of old,
　the Wonders of his Might ;
12 On them my Heart shall meditate,
　my Tongue shall them recite.
13 Safe lodg'd from human Search on high !
　O God, thy Counsels are !
　Who is so great a God as ours ?
　who can with Him compare ?
14 Long since a God of Wonders, Thee
　thy rescu'd People found ;
15 Long since hast Thou thy chosen Seed
　with strong Deliv'rance crown'd.
16 When Thee, O God, the Waters saw,
　the frighted Billows shrunk ;
　The troubled Depths themselves for Fear
　beneath their Channels sunk.
17 The Clouds pour'd down, while rending Skies
　did with their Noise conspire ;
　Thy Arrows all abroad were sent,
　wing'd with avenging Fire.
18 Heav'n with thy Thunder's Voice was torn,
　whilst all the lower World

With Light'nings blaz'd, Earth shook, and seem'd
   from her Foundation hurl'd.
19 Through rolling Streams Thou find'st thy Way,
   thy Paths in Waters lie;
Thy wondrous Passage, where no Sight
   thy Footsteps can descry.
20 Thou led'st thy People like a Flock
   safe through the desert Land,
By *Moses*, their meek skilful Guide,
   and *Aaron's* sacred Hand.

PSALM LXXVIII.

1 HEAR, O my People; to my Law
   devout Attention lend;
Let the Instruction of my Mouth
   deep in your Hearts descend.
2 My Tongue, by Inspiration taught,
   shall Parables unfold,
Dark Oracles, but understood,
   and own'd for Truths of old;
3 Which we from sacred Registers
   of antient Times have known,
And our Forefathers' pious Care
   to us has handed down.
4 We will not hide them from our Sons:
   our Offspring shall be taught
The Praises of the Lord, whose Strength
   has Works of Wonder wrought.
5 For *Jacob* he this Law ordain'd,
   this League with *Israel* made;
With Charge, to be from Age to Age,
   from Race to Race convey'd;
6 That Generations yet to come
   should to their unborn Heirs
Religiously transmit the same,
   and they again to theirs.
7 To teach them that in God alone
   their Hope securely stands;
That they should ne'er his Works forget,
   but keep his just Commands.
8 Lest, like their Fathers, they might prove
   a stiff rebellious Race,

False-hearted, fickle to their God,
  unstedfast in his Grace.
9 Such were revolting *Ephraim's* Sons,
  who, tho' to Warfare bred,
And skilful Archers arm'd with Bows,
  from Field ignobly fled.
10, 11 They falsify'd their League with God,
  his Orders disobey'd,
Forgot his Works and Miracles
  before their Eyes display'd.
12 Nor Wonders, which their Fathers saw,
  did they in Mind retain:
Prodigious Things in *Egypt* done,
  and *Zoan's* fertile Plain.
13 He cut the Seas to let them pass,
  restrain'd the pressing Flood;
While pil'd on Heaps, on either Side,
  the solid Waters stood.
14 A wondrous Pillar led them on,
  compos'd of Shade and Light;
A shelt'ring Cloud it prov'd by Day,
  a leading Fire by Night.
15 When Drought oppress'd 'em, where no Stream
  the Wilderness supply'd,
He cleft the Rock, whose flinty Breast
  dissolv'd into a Tide.
16 Streams from the solid Rock He brought,
  which down in Rivers fell;
That trav'lling with their Camp each Day
  renew'd the Miracle.
17 Yet there they sinn'd against Him more,
  provoking the Most High;
In that same Desert where He did
  their fainting Souls supply.
18 They first incens'd Him in their Hearts,
  that did his Pow'r distrust,
And long'd for Meat, not urg'd by Want,
  but to indulge their Lust.
19 Then utt'ring their blaspheming Doubts;
  " Can God, say they, prepare
  " A Table in the Wilderness,
  " set out with various Fare?

20 " He

PSALM lxxviii.

20 "He smote the flinty Rock ('tis true,)
    "and gushing Streams ensu'd:
    "But can He Corn and Flesh provide
    "for such a Multitude?"
21 The Lord with Indignation heard;
    from Heav'n avenging Flame
    On *Jacob* fell, consuming Wrath
    on thankless *Israel* came:
22 Because their unbelieving Hearts
    in God would not confide;
    Nor trust his Care, who had from Heav'n
    their Wants so oft supply'd.
23 Tho' He had made his Clouds discharge
    Provisions down in Show'rs;
    And, when Earth fail'd, reliev'd their Needs
    from his Celestial Stores.
24 Tho' tasteful Manna was rain'd down
    their Hunger to relieve;
    Tho' from the Stores of Heav'n they did
    sustaining Corn receive.
25 Thus Man with Angels' sacred Food,
    ungrateful Man, was fed;
    Not sparingly, for still they found
    a plenteous Table spread.
26 From Heav'n He made an East-Wind blow,
    then did the South command
27 To rain down Flesh like Dust, and Fowls
    like Seas' unnumber'd Sand.
28 Within their Trenches He let fall
    the luscious easy Prey,
    And all around their spreading Camp
    the feather'd Booty lay.
29 They fed, were fill'd; he gave them Leave
    their Appetites to feast;
30, 31 Yet still their wanton Lust crav'd on,
    nor with their Hunger ceas'd,
    But whilst in their luxurious Mouths
    they did their Dainties chew,
    The Wrath of God smote down their Chiefs,
    and *Israel's* Chosen slew.

PART

PSALM lxxviii.

PART II.

32 Yet still they sinn'd, nor would afford
  his Miracles Belief;
33 Therefore thro' fruitless Travels He
  consum'd their Lives in Grief.
34 When some were slain, the rest return'd
  to God with early Cry:
35 Own'd Him the Rock of their Defence,
  their Saviour, God most High.
36 But this was feign'd Submission all,
  their Heart their Tongue bely'd;
37 Their Heart was still perverse, nor would
  firm in his League abide.
38 Yet, full of Mercy, He forgave,
  nor did with Death chastise;
  But turn'd his kindled Wrath aside,
  or would not let it rise.
39 For He remember'd they were Flesh,
  that could not long remain;
  A murm'ring Wind that's quickly past,
  and ne'er returns again.
40 How oft did they provoke Him there,
  how oft his Patience grieve,
  In that same Desert where He did
  their fainting Souls relieve?
41 They tempted Him by turning back,
  and wickedly repin'd;
  When *Israel's* God refus'd to be
  by their Desires confin'd.
42 Nor call'd to Mind the Hand and Day
  that their Redemption brought;
43 His Signs in *Egypt*, wondrous Works
  in *Zoan's* Valley wrought.
44 He turn'd their Rivers into Blood,
  that Man and Beast forbore;
  And rather chose to die of Thirst,
  than drink the putrid Gore.
45 He sent devouring Swarms of Flies,
  hoarse Frogs annoy'd their Soil,
46 Locusts and Caterpillars reap'd
  the Harvest of their Toil.

47 Their

PSALM lxxviii.

47 Their Vines with batt'ring Hail were broke,
    with Frost the Fig-tree dies;
48 Light'ning and Hail make Flocks and Herds
    one general Sacrifice.
49 He turn'd his Anger loose, and set
    no Time for it to cease;
   And with their Plagues bad Angels sent
    their Torments to increase.
50 He clear'd a Passage for his Wrath
    to ravage uncontrol'd;
   The Murrain on their Firstlings seiz'd
    in ev'ry Field and Fold.
51 The deadly Pest from Beast to Man,
    from Field to City came;
   It flew their Heirs, their eldest Hopes,
    thro' all the Tents of *Ham*.
52 But his own Tribe, like folded Sheep,
    He brought from their Distress;
   And them conducted like a Flock,
    throughout the Wilderness.
53 He led them on, and in their Way
    no Cause of Fear they found;
   But march'd securely thro' those Deeps,
    in which their Foes were drown'd.
54 Nor ceas'd his Care, till them he brought
    safe to his promis'd Land,
   And to his holy Mount the Prize
    of his victorious Hand:
55 To them the out-cast Heathens Land
    He did by Lot divide;
   And in their Foes' abandon'd Tents
    made *Israel's* Tribe reside.

PART III.

56 Yet still they tempted, still provok'd
    the Wrath of God Most High;
   Nor would to practise his Commands
    their stubborn Hearts apply;
57 But in their faithless Fathers' Steps
    perversely chose to go:
   They turn'd aside, like Arrows shot
    from some deceitful Bow.

H   58 For

58 For Him to Fury they provok'd
    with Altars set on high;
   And with their graven Images
    inflam'd his Jealousy.
59 When God heard this, on *Israel's* Tribes
    His Wrath and Hatred fell;
60 He quitted *Shiloh*, and the Tents
    where once he chose to dwell.
61 To vile Captivity his Ark,
    his Glory to disdain,
62 His People to the Sword He gave,
    nor would his Wrath restrain.
63 Destructive War their ablest Youth
    untimely did confound;
   No Virgin was to th' Altar led,
    with Nuptial Garlands crown'd.
64 In Fight the Sacrificer fell,
    the Priest a Victim bled;
   And Widows, who their Deaths should mourn,
    themselves of Grief were dead.
65 Then as a Giant rous'd from Sleep,
    whom Wine had throughly warm'd,
   Shouts out aloud; the Lord awak'd
    and his proud Foe alarm'd.
66 He smote their Host, that from the Field
    a scatter'd Remnant came,
   With Wounds imprinted on their Backs
    of everlasting Shame.
67 With Conquests crown'd, He *Joseph's* Tents
    and *Ephraim's* Tribes forsook;
68 But *Judah* chose, and *Sion's* Mount
    for his lov'd Dwelling took.
69 His Temple He erected there
    with Spires exalted high;
   While deep, and fix'd as that of Earth,
    the strong Foundations lie.
70 His faithful Servant *David* too
    He for his Choice did own,
   And from the Sheep-folds him advanc'd
    to sit on *Judah's* Throne.
71 From tending on the teeming Ewes,
    He brought him forth to feed.

His

His own Inheritance, the Tribes
   of *Israel's* chosen Seed.
72 Exalted thus the Monarch prov'd
   a faithful Shepherd still;
He fed them with an upright Heart,
   and guided them with Skill.

PSALM LXXIX.

1 BEHOLD, O God, how Heathen Hosts
   have thy Possession seiz'd!
Thy sacred House they have defil'd,
   thy holy City raz'd!
2 The mangled Bodies of thy Saints
   abroad unburied lay;
Their Flesh expos'd to savage Beasts,
   and rav'nous Birds of Prey.
3 Quite thro' *Jerus'lem* was their Blood,
   like common Water shed,
And none were left alive to pay
   last Duties to the Dead.
4 The neighb'ring Lands our small Remains
   with loud Reproaches wound;
And we a Laughing-stock are made
   to all the Nations round.
5 How long wilt thou be angry, Lord?
   must we for ever mourn?
Shall thy devouring jealous Rage
   like Fire for ever burn?
6 On Foreign Lands that know not Thee,
   thy heavy Vengeance show'r;
Those sinful Kingdoms let it crush,
   that have not own'd thy Pow'r.
7 For their devouring Jaws have prey'd
   on *Jacob's* chosen Race;
And to a barren Desert turn'd
   their fruitful Dwelling-place.
8 Oh, think not on our former Sins,
   but speedily prevent
The utter Ruin of thy Saints,
   almost with Sorrow spent.
9 Thou God of our Salvation, help,
   and free our Souls from Blame;

PSALM lxxix, lxxx.

 So shall our Pardon and Defence
  exalt thy glorious Name.
10 Let Infidels that scoffing say,
  where is the God they boast?
 In Vengeance for thy slaughter'd Saints,
  perceive Thee to their Cost.
11 Lord, hear the sighing Pris'ners Moans,
  thy saving Power extend;
 Preserve the Wretches doom'd to die,
  from that untimely End.
12 On them, who us oppress, let all
  our Suff'rings be repaid;
 Make their Confusion seven Times more
  than what on us they laid.
13 So we thy People and thy Flock
  shall ever praise thy Name;
 And with glad Hearts our grateful Thanks
  from Age to Age proclaim.

PSALM LXXX.

1 O *Israel's* Shepherd, *Joseph's* Guide,
  Our Prayers to Thee vouchsafe to hear;
 Thou, that dost on the Cherubs ride,
  Again in solemn State appear.
2 Behold how *Benjamin* expects,
  With *Ephraim* and *Manasseh* join'd,
 In our Deliv'rance the Effects
  Of thy resistless Strength to find.
3 Do thou convert us, Lord, do Thou
  The Lustre of thy Face display;
 And all the Ills we suffer now,
  Like scatter'd Clouds, shall pass away.
4 O Thou, whom Heav'nly Hosts obey,
  How long shall thy fierce Anger burn?
 How long thy suff'ring People pray,
  And to their Prayers have no Return?
5 When hungry, we are forc'd to drench
  Our scanty Food in Floods of Woe;
 When dry, our raging Thirst we quench
  With Streams of Tears that largely flow.
6 For us the Heathen Nations round,
  As for a common Prey, contest;

          Our

PSALM lxxx.

Our Foes with spiteful Joy abound,
And at our lost Condition jest.
7 Do Thou convert us, Lord, do Thou
The Lustre of thy Face display,
And all the Ills we suffer now,
Like scatter'd Clouds, shall pass away.

PART II.

8 Thou brought'st a Vine from *Egypt's* Land;
And, casting out the Heathen Race,
Didst plant it with thine own Right-Hand,
And firmly fix'd it in their Place.

9 Before it Thou prepar'dst the Way,
And mad'st it take a lasting Root;
Which, bless'd with thy indulgent Ray,
O'er all the Land did widely shoot.

10, 11 The Hills were cover'd with its Shade,
Its goodly Boughs did Cedars seem :
Its Branches to the Sea were spread,
And reach'd to proud *Euphrates'* Stream.

12 Why then hast Thou its Hedge o'erthrown,
Which Thou hadst made so firm and strong?
Whilst all its Grapes, defenceless grown,
Are pluck'd by those that pass along.

13 See how the bristling Forest Boar
With dreadful Fury lays it waste;
Hark how the savage Monsters roar,
And to their helpless Prey make haste.

PART III.

14 To Thee, O God of Hosts, we pray;
Thy wonted Goodness, Lord, renew:
From Heav'n thy Throne this Vine survey,
And her sad State with Pity view.

15 Behold the Vineyard made by Thee,
Which thy Right-Hand did guard so long;
And keep that Branch from Danger free,
Which for Thyself thou mad'st so strong.

16 To wasting Flames 'tis made a Prey,
And all its spreading Boughs cut down;
At thy Rebuke they soon decay,
And perish at thy dreadful Frown.

17 Crown Thou the King with good Succefs,
   By thy Right-Hand fecur'd from Wrong;
   The Son of Man in Mercy blefs,
   Whom for Thyfelf Thou mad'ft fo ftrong.
18 So fhall we ftill continue free
   From whatfoe'er deferves thy Blame;
   And, if once more reviv'd by Thee,
   Will always praife thy holy Name.
19 Do Thou convert us, Lord, do Thou
   The Luftre of thy Face difplay,
   And all the Ills we fuffer now,
   Like fcatter'd Clouds, fhall pafs away.

PSALM LXXXI.

1 TO God, our never-failing Strength,
     with loud Applaufes fing;
   And jointly make a cheerful Noife
     to *Jacob's* aweful King.
2 Compofe a Hymn of Praife, and touch
     your Inftruments of Joy;
   Let Pfalteries and pleafant Harps
     your grateful Skill employ.
3 Let Trumpets at the great New Moon
     their joyful Voices raife,
   To celebrate th' appointed Time,
     the folemn Day of Praife.
4 For this a Statute was of old,
     which *Jacob's* God decreed,
   To be with pious Care obferv'd
     by *Ifrael's* chofen Seed.
5 This He for a Memorial fix'd,
     when freed from *Egypt's* Land;
   Strange Nations barb'rous Speech we heard,
     but could not underftand.
6 Your burden'd Shoulders I reliev'd,
     (thus feem'd our God to fay)
   Your fervile Hands by Me were freed
     from lab'ring in the Clay.
7 Your Anceftors, with Wrongs opprefs'd,
     to Me for Aid did call:
   With Pity I their Suff'rings faw,
     and fet them free from all.

They

PSALM lxxxi.

They fought for Me, and from the Clouds
   in Thunder I reply'd:
At *Meribah's* contentious Stream
   their Faith and Duty try'd.

PART II.

8 While I my solemn Will declare,
   my chosen People, hear:
If thou, O *Israel*, to my Words
   wilt lend thy list'ning Ear;
9 Then shall no God besides Myself
   within thy Coasts be found;
Nor shalt thou worship any God
   of all the Nations round.
10 The Lord thy God am I, who thee
   brought forth from *Egypt's* Land:
Tis I that all thy just Desires
   supply with lib'ral Hand.
11 But they, my chosen Race, refus'd
   to hearken to my Voice;
Nor would rebellious *Israel's* Sons
   make Me their happy Choice.
12 So I, provok'd, resign'd them up,
   to ev'ry Lust a Prey;
And in their own perverse Designs
   permitted them to stray.
13 O that my People wisely would
   my just Commandments heed!
And *Israel* in my righteous Ways
   with pious Care proceed!
14 Then should my heavy Judgments fall
   on all that them oppose;
And my avenging Hand be turn'd
   against their num'rous Foes.
15 Their Enemies and mine should all
   before my Footstool bend:
But as for them, their happy State
   shall never know an End.
16 All Parts with Plenty shall abound;
   with finest Wheat their Field:
The barren Rocks, to please their Taste,
   should richest Honey yield.

PSALM LXXXII.

1 GOD in the great Assembly stands,
   where his impartial Eye
In State surveys the earthly Gods,
   and does their Judgments try.
2, 3 How dare ye then unjustly judge,
   or be to Sinners kind?
Defend the Orphans and the Poor;
   let such your Justice find.
4 Protect the humble helpless Man,
   reduc'd to deep Distress,
And let not him become a Prey
   to such as would oppress.
5 They neither know, nor will they learn,
   but blindly rove and stray:
Justice and Truth, the World's Support,
   thro' all the Land decay.
6 Well then might God in Anger say,
   " I've call'd ye by my Name:
" I've said, y'are Gods, the Sons and Heirs
   " of my immortal Fame.
7 " But ne'ertheless your unjust Deeds
   " to strict Account I'll call:
" You all shall die like common Men,
   " like other Tyrants fall."
8 Arise, and thy just Judgments, Lord,
   throughout the Earth display;
And all the Nations of the World
   shall own thy righteous Sway.

PSALM LXXXIII.

1 HOLD not thy Peace, O Lord our God,
   no longer silent be;
Nor with consenting quiet Looks
   our Ruin calmly see!
2 For, lo! the Tumults of thy Foes
   o'er all the Land are spread;
And they, which hate thy Saints and Thee,
   lift up their threat'ning Head.
3 Against thy zealous People, Lord,
   they craftily combine;

And

And to deftroy thy chofen Saints
   have laid their clofe Defign.
4 " Come, let us cut them off," fay they,
   " their Nation quite deface;
   " That no Remembrance may remain
   " of *Ifrael's* chofen Race."
5 Thus they againft thy People's Peace
   confult with one Confent;
   And diff'ring Nations, jointly leagu'd,
   their common Malice vent.
6 The *Ifhm'elites* that dwell in Tents,
   with warlike *Edom* join'd;
   And *Moab's* Sons our Ruin vow,
   with *Hagar's* Race combin'd.
7 Proud *Ammon's* Offspring, *Gebal* too,
   with *Amalek* confpire:
   The Lords of *Paleftine*, and all
   the wealthy Sons of *Tyre*.
8 All thefe the ftrong *Affyrian* King
   their firm Ally have got:
   Who with a pow'rful Army aids
   th' inceftuous Race of *Lot*.

PART II.

9 But let fuch Vengeance come to them,
   as once to *Midian* came;
   To *Jabin* and proud *Sifera*,
   at *Kifhon's* fatal Stream.
10 When thy Right-hand their num'rous Hofts
    near *Endor* did confound,
    And left their Carcafes for Dung
    to feed the hungry Ground.
11 Let all their mighty Men the Fate
    of *Zeb* and *Oreb* fhare;
    As *Zeba* and *Zalmunnah*, fo
    let all their Princes fare.
12 Who, with the fame Defign infpir'd,
    thus vainly boafting fpake,
    " In firm Poffeffion for ourfelves
    " let us God's Houfes take."
13 To Ruin let them hafte, like Wheels
    which downward fwiftly move:

                                    Like

Like Chaff before the Winds let all
their scatter'd Forces prove.
14, 15 As Flames confume dry Wood, or Heath
that on parch'd Mountains grows,
So let thy fierce purfuing Wrath
with Terror ftrike thy Foes.
16, 17 Lord, fhroud their Faces with Difgrace,
that they may own thy Name:
Or them confound, whofe harden'd Hearts
thy gentler Means difclaim.
18 So fhall the wond'ring World confefs
that Thou, who claim'ft alone
Jehovah's Name, o'er all the Earth
haft rais'd thy lofty Throne.

PSALM LXXXIV.

1 O God of Hofts, the mighty Lord,
how lovely is the Place
Where Thou, enthron'd in Glory, fhew'ft
the Brightnefs of thy Face!
2 My longing Soul faints with Defire
to view thy bleft Abode:
My panting Heart and Flefh cry out
for Thee the living God.
3 The Birds, more happy far than I,
around thy Temple throng;
Securely there they build, and there
fecurely hatch their Young.
4 O Lord of Hofts, my King and God,
how highly blefs'd are they
Who in thy Temple always dwell,
and there thy Praife difplay!
5 Thrice happy they, whofe Choice has Thee
their fure Protection made;
Who long to tread the facred Ways
that to thy Dwelling lead!
6 Who pafs thro' parch'd and thirfty Vales,
yet no Refrefhment want:
Their Pools are fill'd with Rain, which Thou
at their Requeft does grant.
7 Thus they proceed from Strength to Strength,
and ftill approach more near;

Till

PSALM lxxxiv, lxxxv.

Till all on *Sion's* holy Mount
 before their God appear.
8 O Lord, the mighty God of Hosts,
 my just Requests regard!
Thou God of *Jacob*, let my Prayer
 be still with Favour heard:
9 Behold, O God, for Thou alone
 canst timely Aid dispense:
On thy anointed Servant look;
 be Thou his strong Defence.
10 For, in thy Courts one single Day
 'tis better to attend,
Than, Lord, in any Place besides
 a Thousand Days to spend.
Much rather in God's House will I
 the meanest Office take,
Than in the wealthy Tents of Sin
 my pompous Dwelling make.
11 For, God, who is our Sun and Shield,
 will Grace and Glory give;
And no good Thing will He with-hold
 from them that justly live.
12 Thou God, whom heav'nly Hosts obey,
 how highly bless'd is he,
Whose Hope and Trust, securely plac'd,
 is still repos'd on Thee!

PSALM LXXXV.

1 LORD, Thou hast granted to thy Land
 the Favours we implor'd,
And faithful *Jacob's* captive Race
 most graciously restor'd.
2,3 Thy People's Sins Thou hast absolv'd,
 and all their Guilt defac'd:
Thou hast not let thy Wrath flame on,
 nor thy fierce Anger last.
4 O God, our Saviour, all our Hearts
 to thy Obedience turn;
That quench'd with our repenting Tears,
 thy Wrath no more may burn.
5,6 For why should'st Thou be angry still
 and Wrath so long retain?

Revive

    Revive us, Lord, and let thy Saints
       thy wonted Comfort gain.
7 Thy gracious Favour, Lord, display,
       which we have long implor'd;
    And, for thy wondrous Mercy's Sake,
       thy wonted Aid afford.
8 God's Answer patiently I'll wait;
       for He, with good Success,
    (If they no more to Folly turn)
       his mourning Saints will bless.
9 To all that fear his holy Name
       his sure Salvation's near;
    And in its former happy State
       our Nation shall appear.
10 For Mercy now with Truth is join'd,
       and Righteousness with Peace;
    Like kind Companions, absent long,
       with friendly Arms embrace.   [Heav'n
11, 12 Truth from the Earth shall spring, whilst
       shall Streams of Justice pour;
    And God, from whom all Goodness flows,
       shall endless Plenty show'r.
13 Before Him Righteousness shall march
       and his just Paths prepare;
    Whilst we his holy Steps pursue
       with constant Zeal and Care.

PSALM LXXXVI.

1 TO my Complaint, O Lord my God,
       thy gracious Ear incline;
    Hear me, distress'd, and destitute
       of all Relief but thine;
2 Do Thou, O God, preserve my Soul,
       that does thy Name adore:
    Thy Servant keep, and him, whose Trust
       relies on Thee, restore.
3 To me, who daily Thee invoke,
       thy Mercy, Lord, extend;
4 Refresh thy Servant's Soul, whose Hopes
       on Thee alone depend.
5 Thou, Lord, art good; not only good,
       but prompt to pardon too:

PSALM lxxxvi.

 Of plenteous Mercy to all thofe
  who for thy Mercy fue.
6 To my repeated humble Prayer,
  O Lord, attentive be;
7 When troubled, I on Thee will call,
  for Thou wilt anfwer me.
8 Among the Gods there's none like Thee,
  O Lord, alone divine!
 To Thee as much inferior they,
  as are their Works to Thine.
9 Therefore their great Creator Thee
  the Nations fhall adore:
 Their long mifguided Prayers and Praife
  to thy blefs'd Name reftore.
10 All fhall confefs Thee great, and great
  the Wonders Thou haft done;
 Confefs Thee God, the God fupreme,
  confefs Thee God alone.

PART II.

11 Teach me thy Way, O Lord, and I
  from Truth fhall ne'er depart;
 In Rev'rence to thy facred Name
  devoutly fix my Heart.
12 Thee will I praife, O Lord my God,
  praife Thee with Heart fincere:
 And to thy everlafting Name
  eternal Trophies rear.
13 Thy boundlefs Mercy fhewn to me
  tranfcends my Pow'r to tell;
 For Thou haft oft redeem'd my Soul
  from loweft Depths of Hell.
14 O God, the Sons of Pride and Strife
  have my Deftruction fought,
 Regardlefs of thy Pow'r, that oft
  has my Deliv'rance wrought:
15 But Thou thy conftant Goodnefs didft
  to my Affiftance bring;
 Of Patience, Mercy, and of Truth,
  thou everlafting Spring!
16 O bounteous Lord, thy Grace and Strength
  to me thy Servant fhow:

PSALM lxxxvi, lxxxvii, lxxxviii.

Thy kind Protection, Lord, on me,
  thine Handmaid's Son, bestow.
17 Some Signal give, which my proud Foes
    may see with Shame and Rage,
  When Thou, O Lord, for my Relief
    and Comfort dost engage.

PSALM LXXXVII.

1 GOD's Temple crowns the holy Mount:
    the Lord there condescends to dwell;
2 His *Sion's* Gates, in his Account,
    our *Israel's* fairest Tents excel.
3 Fame glorious Things of Thee shall sing,
    O City of the Almighty King!
4 I'll mention *Rahab* with due Praise,
    in *Babylon's* Applauses join,
  The Fame of *Ethiopia* raise,
    with that of *Tyre* and *Palestine*;
  And grant that some, amongst them born,
    Their Age and Country did adorn.
5 But still of *Sion* I'll aver,
    that many such from her proceed;
  Th' Almighty shall establish her.
6 His gen'ral List shall shew, when read,
    That such a Person there was born,
  And such did such an Age adorn.
7 He'll *Sion* find with Numbers fill'd
    of such as merit high Renown;
  For Hand and Voice Musicians skill'd;
    and (her transceding Fame to crown)
  Of such she shall Successions bring,
  Like Waters from a living Spring.

PSALM LXXXVIII.

1 TO Thee, my God and Saviour, I
    By Day and Night address my Cry:
2 Vouchsafe my mournful Voice to hear;
  To my Distress incline thine Ear:
3 For Seas of Trouble me invade,
  My Soul draws nigh to Death's cold Shade.
4 Like one whose Strength and Hopes are fled,
  They number me among the Dead.

PSALM lxxxviii.

5 Like those who, shrouded in the Grave,
  From Thee no more Remembrance have;
6 Cast off from thy sustaining Care,
  Down to the Confines of Despair.
7 Thy Wrath has hard upon me lain,
  Afflicting me with restless Pain;
  Me all thy Mountain Waves have prest,
  Too weak, alas, to bear the least.
8 Remov'd from Friends, I sigh alone,
  In a loath'd Dungeon laid, where none
  A Visit will vouchsafe to me,
  Confin'd, past Hopes of Liberty.
9 My Eyes from weeping never cease,
  They waste, but still my Griefs increase;
  Yet daily, Lord, to Thee I've pray'd,
  With out-stretch'd Hand invok'd thy Aid.
10 Wilt Thou by Miracles revive
  The Dead, whom Thou forsook'st alive?
  From Death restore, thy Praise to sing,
  Whom Thou from Prison would'st not bring?
11 Shall the mute Grave thy Love confess?
  A mould'ring Tomb thy Faithfulness?
12 Thy Truth and Power Renown obtain,
  Where Darkness and Oblivion reign?
13 To Thee, O Lord, I cry forlorn;
  My Prayer prevents the early Morn.
14 Why hast Thou, Lord, my Soul forsook,
  Nor once vouchsaf'd a gracious Look?
15 Prevailing Sorrows bear me down,
  Which from my Youth with me have grown:
  Thy Terrors past distract my Mind,
  And Fears of blacker Days behind.
16 Thy Wrath has burst upon my Head,
  Thy Terrors fill my Soul with Dread;
17 Environ'd as with Waves combin'd,
  And for a gen'ral Deluge join'd.
18 My Lovers, Friends, Familiars, all
  Remov'd from Sight, and out of Call;
  To dark Oblivion all retir'd,
  Dead, or at least to me expir'd.

PSALM

PSALM LXXXIX.

1 THY Mercies, Lord, shall be my Song,
  My Song on them shall ever dwell;
  To Ages yet unborn my Tongue
  Thy never-failing Truth shall tell.

2 I have affirm'd, and still maintain,
  Thy Mercy shall for ever last;
  Thy Truth, that does the Heavens sustain,
  Like them shall stand for ever fast.

3 Thus spak'st Thou by the Prophet's Voice,
  " With *David* I a League have made;
  " To him, my Servant, and my Choice,
  " By solemn Oaths this Grant convey'd;

4 " While Earth, and Seas, and Skies, endure,
  " Thy Seed shall in my Sight remain;
  " To them thy Throne I will ensure,
  " They shall to endless Ages reign."

5 For such stupendous Truth and Love
  Both Heaven and Earth just Praises owe,
  By Choirs of Angels sung above,
  And by assembled Saints below.

6 What Seraph of celestial Birth,
  To vie with *Israel's* God shall dare?
  Or who among the Gods of Earth
  With our Almighty Lord compare?

7 With Rev'rence and religious Dread
  His Saints should to his Temple press:
  His Fear thro' all their Hearts should spread,
  Who his Almighty Name confess.

8 Lord God of Armies, who can boast
  Of Strength or Power like thine renown'd?
  Of such a num'rous faithful Host,
  As that which does thy Throne surround;

9 Thou dost the lawless Sea control,
  And change the Prospect of the Deep;
  Thou mak'st the sleeping Billows roll,
  Thou mak'st the rolling Billows sleep.

10 Thou brak'st in Pieces *Rahab's* Pride,
   And didst oppressing Power disarm;
   Thy scatter'd Foes have dearly try'd
   The Force of thy resistless Arm.

PSALM lxxxix.

11 In Thee the fov'reign Right remains
    Of Earth and Heav'n: Thee, Lord, alone,
    The World, and all that it contains,
    Their Maker and Preserver own.
12 The Poles on which the Globe does reft
    Were form'd by thy creating Voice;
    Tabor and *Hermon*, Eaft and Weft,
    In thy fuftaining Pow'r rejoice.
13 Thy Arm is mighty, ftrong thy Hand,
    Yet, Lord, Thou doft with Juftice reign;
14 Poffefs'd of abfolute Command,
    Thou Truth and Mercy doft maintain.
15 Happy, thrice happy, they who hear
    Thy facred Trumpet's joyful found;
    Who may at Feftivals appear
    With thy moft glorious Prefence crown'd.
16 Thy Saints fhall always be o'erjoy'd,
    Who on thy facred Name rely;
    And, in thy Righteoufnefs employ'd,
    Above their Foes be rais'd on high.
17 For in thy Strength they fhall advance,
    Whofe Conquefts from thy Favour fpring;
18 The Lord of Hofts is our Defence,
    And *Ifrael's* God our *Ifrael's* King.
19 Thus fpak'ft Thou by thy Prophet's Voice,
    " A mighty Champion I will fend:
    " From *Judah's* Tribe have I made Choice
    " Of one who fhall the reft defend.
20 " My Servant *David* I have found,
    " With holy Oil anointed him;
21 " Him fhall the Hand fupport that crown'd,
    " And guard that gave the Diadem.
22 " No Prince from him fhall Tribute force,
    " No Son of Strife fhall him annoy;
23 " His fpiteful Foes I will difperfe,
    " And them before his Face deftroy.
24 " My Truth and Grace fhall him fuftain;
    " His Armies, in well-order'd Ranks,
25 " Shall conquer, from the *Tyrian* Main
    " To *Tygris* and *Euphrates*' Banks.
26 " Me for his Father he fhall take,
    " His God and Rock of Safety call;

I   27 " Him

27 " Him I my firſt-born Son will make,
   " And earthly Kings his Subjects all.
28 " To him my Mercy I'll ſecure,
   " My Cov'nant make for ever faſt;
29 " His Seed for ever ſhall endure,
   " His Throne, till Heav'n diſſolves, ſhall laſt.

PART II.

30 " But if his Heirs my Law forſake,
   " And from my ſacred Precepts ſtray;
31 " If they my righteous Statutes break,
   " Nor ſtrictly my Commands obey;
32 " Their Sins I'll viſit with a Rod,
   " And for their Folly make them ſmart;
33 " Yet will not ceaſe to be their God,
   " Nor from my Truth, like them, depart.
34 " My Cov'nant I will ne'er revoke,
   " But in Remembrance faſt retain;
   " The Thing, that once my Lips have ſpoke,
   " Shall in eternal Force remain.
35 " Once have I ſworn, but once for all,
   " And made my Holineſs the Tie,
   " That I my Grant will ne'er recal,
   " Nor to my Servant *David* lie.
36 " Whoſe Throne and Race the conſtant Sun
   " Shall, like his Courſe, eſtabliſh'd ſee:
37 " Of this my Oath, thou conſcious Moon,
   " In Heav'n my faithful Witneſs be."
38 Such was thy gracious Promiſe, Lord;
   But thou haſt now our Tribes forſook,
   Thy own Anointed haſt abhorr'd,
   And turn'd on him thy wrathful Look.
39 Thou ſeemeſt to have render'd void
   The Cov'nant with thy Servant made,
   Thou haſt his Dignity deſtroy'd,
   And in the Duſt his Honour laid.
40 Of Strong-holds Thou haſt him bereft,
   And brought his Bulwarks to decay;
41 His Frontier Coaſts defenceleſs left,
   A public Scorn and common Prey.
42 His Ruin does glad Triumphs yield
   To Foes advanc'd by Thee to Might:

43 Thou haſt his conqu'ring-Sword unſteel'd,
　His Valour turn'd to ſhameful Flight.
44 His Glory is to Darkneſs fled,
　His Throne is level'd with the Ground;
45 His Youth to wretched Bondage led,
　With Shame o'erwhelm'd and Sorrow drown'd.
46 How long ſhall we thy Abſence mourn?
　Wilt Thou for ever, Lord, retire?
　Shall thy conſuming Anger burn,
　Till that and we at once expire?
47 Conſider, Lord, how ſhort a Space
　Thou doſt for mortal Life ordain;
　No Method to prolong the Race,
　But loading it with Grief and Pain.
48 What Man is he that can control
　Death's ſtrict unalterable Doom?
　Or reſcue from the Grave his Soul,
　The Grave that muſt Mankind entomb?
49 Lord, where's thy Love, thy boundleſs Grace,
　The Oath to which thy Truth did ſeal,
　Conſign'd to *David* and his Race,
　The Grant which Time ſhould ne'er repeal?
50 See how thy Servants treated are
　With Infamy, Reproach, and Spite;
　Which in my ſilent Breaſt I bear
　From Nations of licentious Might.
51 How they, reproaching thy great Name,
　Have made thy Servants' Hope their Jeſt:
52 Yet thy juſt Praiſes we'll proclaim,
　And ever ſing, *The Lord be bleſt.*

　　　　　　　　　　　Amen, Amen.

PSALM XC.

1 O LORD, the Saviour and Defence
　　of us thy choſen Race,
　From Age to Age Thou ſtill haſt been
　　our ſure Abiding Place.
2 Before Thou brought'ſt the Mountains forth,
　　or th' Earth and World didſt frame,
　Thou always wert the mighty God,
　　and ever art the ſame.

3 Thou turnest Man, O Lord, to Dust,
   of which he first was made;
  And when Thou speak'st the Word *Return*,
   'tis instantly obey'd.
4 For in thy Sight a thousand Years
   are like a Day that 's past,
  Or like a Watch in Dead of Night,
   whose Hours unminded waste.
5 Thou sweep'st us off as with a Flood,
   we vanish hence like Dreams;
  At first we grow like Grass that feels
   the Sun's reviving Beams:
6 But, howsoever fresh and fair
   its Morning Beauty shows;
  'Tis all cut down, and wither'd quite,
   before the Evening close.
7, 8 We by thine Anger are consum'd,
   and by thy Wrath dismay'd;
  Our public Crimes and secret Sins
   before thy Sight are laid.
9 Beneath thy Anger's sad Effects
   our drooping Days we spend;
  Our unregarded Years break off,
   like Tales that quickly end.
10 Our Term of Time is Seventy Years,
   an Age that few survive:
  But if, with more than common Strength,
   to Eighty we arrive;
  Yet then our boasted Strength decays,
   to Sorrow turn'd and Pain:
  So soon the slender Thread is cut,
   and we no more remain.

PART II.

11 But who thy Anger's dread Effects
   does, as he ought, revere?
  And yet thy Wrath doth fall or rise,
   as more or less we fear.
12 So teach us, Lord, th' uncertain Sum
   of our short Days to mind,
  That to true Wisdom all our Hearts
   may ever be inclin'd.

13 O to thy Servants, Lord, return,
and speedily relent!
As we of our Misdeeds, do Thou
of our just Doom repent.
14 To satisfy and cheer our Souls
Thy early Mercy send;
That we may all our Days to come
in Joy and Comfort spend;
15 Let happy Times with large Amends
dry up our former Tears,
Or equal at the least the Term
of our afflicted Years.
16 To all thy Servants, Lord, let this
thy wondrous Work be known,
And to our Offspring yet unborn
thy glorious Pow'r be shown.
17 Let thy bright Rays upon us shine,
give Thou our Work Success;
The glorious Work we have in Hand
do thou vouchsafe to bless.

PSALM XCI.

1 HE that has God his Guardian made
Shall, under the Almighty's Shade,
secure and undisturb'd abide.
2 Thus to my Soul of Him I'll say,
He is my Fortress and my Stay,
my God in whom I will confide.
3 His tender Love and watchful Care
Shall free thee from the Fowler's Snare,
and from the noisome Pestilence:
4 He over thee his Wings shall spread,
And cover thy unguarded Head;
his Truth shall be thy strong Defence.
5 No Terrors that surprize by Night
Shall thy undaunted Courage fright,
nor deadly Shafts that fly by Day;
6 Nor Plague of unknown Rise, that kills
In Darkness, nor infectious Ills
that in the hottest Season slay.
7 A Thousand at thy Side shall die,
At thy Right-hand Ten Thousand lie,
while thy firm Health untouch'd remains:

8 Thou only shalt look on, and see
 The Wicked's sad Catastrophe,
  and count the Sinner's mournful Gains.
9 Because (with well-plac'd Confidence)
 Thou mak'st the Lord thy sure Defence,
  and on the Highest dost rely;
10 Therefore no Ill shall thee befal,
 Nor to thy healthful Dwelling shall
  any infectious Plague draw nigh.
11 For He, throughout thy happy Days,
 To keep thee safe in all thy Ways
  shall give his Angels strict Commands;
12 And they, lest thou should'st chance to meet
 With some rough Stone to wound thy Feet,
  shall bear thee safely in their Hands.
13 Dragons and Asps that thirst for Blood,
 And Lions roaring for their Food,
  beneath his conqu'ring Feet shall lie.
14 Because he lov'd and honour'd Me,
 Therefore, says God, I'll set him free,
  and fix his Throne on high.
15 He'll call; I'll answer when he calls,
 And rescue him when Ill befalls;
  increase his Honour and his Wealth:
16 And when, with undisturb'd Content,
 His long and happy Life is spent,
  his End I'll crown with saving Health.

PSALM XCII.

1 HOW good and pleasant must it be
  to thank the Lord most high;
 And with repeated Hymns of Praise
  his Name to magnify!
2 With ev'ry Morning's early Dawn
  his Goodness to relate;
 And of his constant Truth, each Night,
  the glad Effects repeat!
3 To ten-string'd Instruments we'll sing,
  with tuneful Psalt'ries join'd;
 And to the Harp, with solemn Sounds,
  for sacred Use design'd.

4 For thro' thy wondrous Works, O Lord,
   Thou mak'ſt my Heart rejoice;
   The Thoughts of them ſhall make me glad,
   and ſhout with cheerful Voice.
5, 6 How wondrous are thy Works, O Lord,
   how deep are thy Decrees!
   Whoſe winding Tracks, in ſecret laid,
   no ſtupid Sinner ſees.
7 He little thinks, when wicked Men,
   like Grafs look freſh and gay,
   How ſoon their ſhort-liv'd Splendor muſt
   for ever paſs away.
8, 9 But thou, my God, art ſtill moſt High;
   and all thy lofty Foes,
   Who thought they might ſecurely ſin,
   ſhall be o'erwhelm'd with Woes:
10 Whilſt Thou exalt'ſt my ſov'reign Pow'r,
   and mak'ſt it largely ſpread;
   And with refreſhing Oil anoint'ſt
   my conſecrated Head.
11 I ſoon ſhall ſee my ſtubborn Foes
   to utter Ruin brought;
   And hear the diſmal End of thoſe
   who have againſt me fought.
12 But righteous Men, like fruitful Palms,
   ſhall make a glorious Show;
   As Cedars that on *Lebanon*
   in ſtately Order grow.
13, 14 Theſe, planted in the Houſe of God,
   within his Courts ſhall thrive;
   Their Vigour and their Luſtre both
   ſhall in old Age revive.
15 Thus will the Lord his Juſtice ſhew;
   and God, my ſtrong Defence,
   Shall due Rewards to all the World
   impartially diſpenſe.

PSALM XCIII.

1 WITH Glory clad, with Strength array'd,
   the Lord, that o'er all Nature reigns,
The World's Foundations ſtrongly laid,
   and the vaſt Fabric ſtill ſuſtains.

2 How surely 'stablish'd is thy Throne!
   which shall no Change or Period see;
   For Thou, O Lord, and Thou alone,
   art God from all Eternity.
3, 4 The Floods, O Lord, lift up their Voice,
   and toss the troubled Waves on high;
   But God above can still their Noise,
   and make the angry Sea comply.
5 Thy Promise, Lord, is ever sure,
   and they that in thy House would dwell,
   That happy Station to secure,
   must still in Holiness excel.

PSALM XCIV.

1, 2 O GOD, to whom Revenge belongs,
   thy Justice now disclose:
   Arise, Thou Judge of all the Earth,
   and crush thy haughty Foes.
3, 4 How long, O Lord, shall sinful Men
   their solemn Triumphs make?
   How long their wicked Actions boast,
   and insolently speak?
5, 6 Not only they thy Saints oppress,
   but, unprovok'd, they spill
   The Widow's and the Stranger's Blood,
   and helpless Orphans kill.
7 "And yet the Lord shall ne'er perceive,"
   (profanely thus they speak)
   "Nor any Notice of our Deeds
   "the God of *Jacob* take."
8 At length, ye stupid Fools, your Wants
   endeavour to discern;
   In Folly will you still proceed,
   and Wisdom never learn?
9, 10 Can He be deaf who form'd the Ear,
   or blind who fram'd the Eye?
   Shall Earth's great Judge not punish those,
   who his known Will defy?
11 He fathoms all the Thoughts of Men,
   to Him their Hearts lie bare;
   His Eye surveys them all, and sees
   how vain their Counsels are.

PSALM xciv.
PART II.

12 Bless'd is the Man whom Thou, O Lord,
  in Kindness dost chastise,
And by thy sacred Rules to walk
  dost lovingly advise.
13 This Man shall Rest and Safety find
  in Seasons of Distress:
Whilst God prepares a Pit for those
  that stubbornly transgress.
14 For God will never from his Saints
  his Favour wholly take;
His own Possession and his Lot
  He will not quite forsake.
15 The World shall then confess Thee just
  in all that Thou hast done;
And those that chuse thy upright Ways
  shall in those Paths go on.
16 Who will appear in my Behalf,
  when wicked Men invade?
Or who, when Sinners would oppress,
  my righteous Cause shall plead?
17, 18, 19 Long since had I in Silence slept,
  but that the Lord was near,
To stay me when I slipt; when sad,
  my troubled Heart to cheer.
20 Wilt Thou, who art a God most just,
  their sinful Throne sustain,
Who make the Law a fair Pretence
  their wicked Ends to gain?
21 Against the Lives of righteous Men
  they form their close Design;
The Blood of Innocents to spill
  in solemn League combine.
22 But my Defence is firmly plac'd
  in God the Lord most High;
He is my Rock to which I may
  for Refuge always fly.
23 The Lord shall cause their ill Design
  on their own Heads to fall:
He in their Sins shall cut them off;
  our God shall slay them all.

PSALM

PSALM XCV.

1 O COME, loud Anthems let us sing,
    Loud Thanks to our Almighty King;
  For we our Voices high should raise,
  When our Salvation's Rock we praise.

2 Into his Presence let us haste,
  To thank him for his Favours past;
  To him address, in joyful Songs,
  The Praise that to his Name belongs.

3 For God the Lord, enthron'd in State,
  Is, with unrival'd Glory, great:
  A King superior far to all,
  Whom by his Title God we call.

4 The Depths of Earth are in his Hand,
  Her secret Wealth at his Command;
  The Strength of Hills that reach the Skies
  Subjected to his Empire lies.

5 The rolling Ocean's vast Abyss
  By the same Sov'reign Right is his:
  'Tis mov'd by his Almighty Hand,
  That form'd and fix'd the solid Land.

6 O let us to his Courts repair,
  And bow with Adoration there:
  Down on our Knees devoutly all
  Before the Lord our Maker fall.

7 For he's our God, our Shepherd He,
  His Flock and Pasture Sheep are we.
  If then you'll (like his Flock) draw near,
  To-day if you his Voice will hear,

8 Let not your harden'd Hearts renew
  Your Fathers Crimes and Judgments too;
  Nor here provoke my Wrath, as they
  In desert Plains of *Meribah*,

9 When thro' the Wilderness they mov'd,
  And me with fresh Temptations prov'd:
  They still thro' Unbelief rebell'd,
  While they my wondrous Works beheld.

10, 11 They Forty Years my Patience griev'd,
  Tho' daily I their Wants reliev'd.
  Then—'Tis a faithless Race I said,
  Whose Heart from me has always stray'd;

They

They ne'er will tread my righteous Path:
Therefore to them, in settled Wrath,
Since they despis'd my Rest, I sware,
That they should never enter there.

PSALM XCVI.

1 SING to the Lord a new-made Song;
  Let Earth, in one assembled Throng,
    Her common Patron's Praise resound.
2 Sing to the Lord, and bless his Name,
  From Day to Day his Praise proclaim,
    Who us has with Salvation crown'd.
3 To Heathen Lands his Fame rehearse,
  His Wonders to the Universe.
4 He's great, and greatly to be prais'd;
  In Majesty and Glory rais'd
    Above all other Deities.
5 For Pageantry and Idols all
  Are they whom Gods the Heathen call:
    He only rules who made the Skies.
6 With Majesty and Honour crown'd,
  Beauty and Strength his Throne surround:
7 Be therefore both to Him restor'd
  By you, who have false Gods ador'd;
    Ascribe due Honour to his Name:
8 Peace-off'rings on his Altar lay,
  Before his Throne your Homage pay,
    Which He, and He alone can claim.
9 To worship at his sacred Court
  Let all the trembling World resort.
10 Proclaim aloud, Jehovah reigns,
  Whose Pow'r the Universe sustains,
    And banish'd Justice will restore.
11 Let, therefore, Heav'n new Joys confess,
  And heav'nly Mirth let Earth express;
    Its loud Applause the Ocean roar;
  Its mute Inhabitants rejoice,
  And for this Triumph find a Voice.
12 For Joy let fertile Vallies sing,
  The cheerful Groves their Tribute bring;
    The tuneful Choir of Birds awake,

13 The

13 The Lord's Approach to celebrate,
Who now fets out with awful State
His Circuit thro' the Earth to take.
From Heav'n to judge the World He's come,
With Juftice to reward and doom.

PSALM XCVII.

1 JEHOVAH reigns, let all the Earth
In his juft Government rejoice;
Let all the Ifles with facred Mirth
In his Applaufe unite their Voice.
2 Darknefs and Clouds of awful Shade
His dazzling Glory fhroud in State:
Juftice and Truth his Guards are made,
And fix'd by his Pavilion wait.
3 Devouring Fire before his Face
His Foes around with Vengeance ftruck:
4 His Lightnings fet the World on Blaze,
Earth faw it, and with Terror fhook.
5 The proudeft Hills his Prefence felt,
Their Height nor Strength could Help afford;
The proudeft Hills like Wax did melt
In Prefence of th' Almighty Lord.
6 The Heav'ns, his Righteoufnefs to fhew,
With Storms of Fire our Foes purfu'd;
And all the trembling World below
Have his defcending Glory view'd.
7 Confounded be their impious Hoft,
Who make the Gods to whom they pray;
All who of Pageant Idols boaft,
To him, ye Gods, your Worfhip pay.
8 Glad *Sion* of thy Triumph heard,
And *Judah's* Daughters were o'erjoy'd;
Becaufe thy righteous Judgments, Lord,
Have Pagan Pride and Pow'r deftroy'd.
9 For thou, O God, art feated high;
Above Earth's Potentates enthron'd:
Thou, Lord, unrival'd in the Sky,
Supreme by all the Gods art own'd.
10 You who to ferve this Lord afpire,
Abhor what's ill, and Truth efteem:

He'll

PSALM xcvii, xcviii.

He'll keep his Servants Souls entire,
And them from wicked Hands redeem.
11 For Seeds are sown of glorious Light,
A future Harvest for the Just;
And Gladness for the Heart that's right,
To recompense its pious Trust.
12 Rejoice, ye Righteous, in the Lord;
Memorials of his Holiness
Deep in your faithful Breasts record,
And with your thankful Tongues confess.

PSALM XCVIII.

1 SING to the Lord a new-made Song,
   who wondrous Things has done;
With his Right-hand and holy Arm
   the Conquest He has won.
2 The Lord has thro' th' astonish'd World
   display'd his saving Might,
And made his righteous Acts appear
   in all the Heathens Sight.
3 Of *Israel's* House his Love and Truth
   have ever mindful been;
Wide Earth's remotest Parts the Pow'r
   of *Israel's* God have seen.
4 Let therefore Earth's Inhabitants
   their cheerful Voices raise,
And all with universal Joy
   resound their Maker's Praise.
5 With Harp and Hymns soft Melody
   into the Concert bring
6 The Trumpet and shrill Cornet's Sound
   before th' Almighty King.
7 Let the loud Ocean roar her Joy,
   with all that Seas contain:
The Earth and her Inhabitants
   join Concert with the Main.
8 With Joy let Riv'lets swell to Streams,
   to spreading Torrents they;
And echoing Vales, from Hill to Hill,
   redoubled Shouts convey;
9 To welcome down the World's great Judge,
   who does with Justice come,

And

And with impartial Equity,
  both to reward and doom.

PSALM XCIX.

1 JEHOVAH reigns, let therefore all
    the guilty Nations quake :
  On Cherubs' Wings he sits enthron'd ;
    let Earth's Foundation shake.
2 On *Sion's* Hill He keeps his Court,
    his Palace makes her Tow'rs ;
  Yet thence his Sov'reignty extends
    supreme o'er earthly Pow'rs.
3 Let therefore all with Praise address,
    his great and dreadful Name,
  And with his unresisted Might
    his Holiness proclaim.
4 For Truth and Justice, in his Reign,
    of Strength and Pow'r take Place ;
  His Judgments are with Righteousness
    dispens'd to *Jacob's* Race.
5 Therefore exalt the Lord our God,
    before his Footstool fall ;
  And with his unresisted Might
    his Holiness extol.
6 *Moses* and *Aaron* thus of old
    among his Priests ador'd ;
  Among his Prophets *Samuel* thus
    his sacred Name implor'd.
  Distress'd, upon the Lord they call'd,
    who ne'er their Suit deny'd ;
  But, as with Rev'rence they implor'd,
    He graciously reply'd.
7 For, with their Camp, to guide their March
    the cloudy Pillar mov'd ;
  They kept his Laws, and to his Will
    obedient Servants prov'd.
8 He answer'd them, forgiving oft
    his People for their Sake ;
  And those who rashly them oppos'd
    did sad Examples make.
9 With Worship at his sacred Courts,
    exalt our God and Lord ;

For He, who only holy is,
 alone should be ador'd.

PSALM C.

1, 2 WITH one Consent let all the Earth
   to God their cheerful Voices raise;
 Glad Homage pay with awful Mirth,
  and sing before Him Songs of Praise.
3 Convinc'd that He is God alone,
  from whom both we and all proceed,
 We, whom he chuses for his own,
  the Flock that he vouchsafes to feed.
4 Oh, enter then his Temple Gate,
  thence to his Courts devoutly press,
 And still your grateful Hymns repeat,
  And still his Name with Praises bless.
5 For He's the Lord supremely good,
  His Mercy is for ever sure;
 His Truth, which always firmly stood,
  to endless Ages shall endure.

PSALM CI.

1 OF Mercy's never-failing Spring,
  And stedfast Judgment, I will sing;
 And since they both to Thee belong,
 To Thee, O Lord, address my Song.
2 When, Lord, Thou shalt with me reside,
 Wise Discipline my Reign shall guide;
 With blameless Life myself I'll make
 A Pattern for my Court to take.
3 No ill Design will I pursue,
 Nor those my Fav'rites make that do.
4 Who to Reproof have no Regard,
 Him will I totally discard.
5 The private Slanderer shall be
 In public Justice doom'd by me:
 From haughty Looks I'll turn aside,
 And mortify the Heart of Pride.
6 But Honesty, call'd from her Cell,
 In Splendor at my Court shall dwell:
 Who Virtue's Practice make their Care
 Shall have the first Preferments there.

7 No Politicks shall recommend
 His Country's Foe to be my Friend:
 None e'er shall to my Favour rise
 By flatt'ring or malicious Lies.
8 All those who wicked Courses take
 An early Sacrifice I'll make:
 Cut off, destroy, till none remain
 God's holy City to prophane.

PSALM CII.

1 WHEN I pour out my Soul in Pray'r,
  do Thou, O Lord, attend;
 To thy eternal Throne of Grace
  let my sad Cry ascend.
2 O hide not Thou thy glorious Face
  in Times of deep Distress;
 Incline thine Ear, and, when I call,
  my Sorrows soon redress.
3 Each cloudy Portion of my Life
  like scatter'd Smoke expires:
 My shrivel'd Bones are like a Hearth,
  that's parch'd with constant Fires.
4 My Heart, like Grass that feels the Blast
  of some infectious Wind,
 Does languish so with Grief, that scarce
  my needful Food I mind.
5 By Reason of my sad Estate,
  I spend my Breath in Groans:
 My Flesh is worn away, my Skin
  scarce hides my starting Bones.
6 I'm like a Pelican become,
  that does in Deserts mourn:
 Or like an Owl, that sits all Day
  on barren Trees forlorn.
7 In Watchings or in restless Dreams
  the Night by me is spent,
 As by those solitary Birds
  that lonesome Roofs frequent.
8 All Day by railing Foes I'm made
  the Subject of their Scorn;
 Who all, possess'd with furious Rage,
  have my Destruction sworn.

9 When

PSALM cii.

9 When grov'ling on the Ground I lie,
    oppress'd with Grief and Fears;
  My Bread is strew'd with Ashes o'er,
    my Drink is mix'd with Tears.
10 Because on me with double Weight
    thy heavy Wrath doth lie;
  For Thou, to make my Fall more great,
    didst lift me up on high.
11 My Days, just hast'ning to their End,
    are like an Ev'ning Shade :
  My Beauty does, like wither'd Grass,
    my waning Lustre fade.
12 But thy eternal State, O Lord,
    no Length of Time shall waste :
  The Mem'ry of thy wondrous Works
    from Age to Age shall last.
13 Thou shalt arise, and *Sion* view
    with an unclouded Face:
  For now her Time is come, thy own
    appointed Day of Grace.
14 Her scatter'd Ruins by thy Saints
    with Pity are survey'd :
  They grieve to see her lofty Spires
    in Dust and Rubbish laid.
15,16 The Name and Glory of the Lord
    all Heathen Kings shall fear;
  When He shall *Sion* build again,
    and in full State appear.
17,18 When He regards the Poor's Request,
    nor slights their earnest Pray'r;
  Our Sons, for this recorded Grace,
    shall his just Praise declare.
19 For God, from his Abode on high,
    his gracious Beams display'd :
  The Lord from Heav'n, his lofty Throne,
    hath all the Earth survey'd.
20 He listen'd to the Captives Moans,
    He heard their mournful Cry,
  And freed, by his resistless Pow'r,
    the Wretches doom'd to die.
21 That they, in *Sion* where He dwells,
    might celebrate his Fame,

K   And

And thro' the holy City sing
  loud Praises to his Name,
22 When all the Tribes assembling there
  their solemn Vows address,
  And neighb'ring Lands with glad Consent
  the Lord their God confess.
23 But, ere my Race is run, my Strength
  through his fierce Wrath decays;
  He has, when all my Wishes bloom'd,
  cut short my hopeful Days.
24 Lord, end not Thou my Life, said I,
  when Half is scarcely past;
  Thy Years, from worldly Changes free,
  to endless Ages last.
25 The strong Foundations of the Earth
  of old by Thee were laid;
  Thy Hands the beauteous Arch of Heav'n
  with wondrous Skill have made:
26, 27 Whilst Thou for ever shalt endure,
  they soon shall pass away;
  And, like a Garment often worn,
  shall tarnish and decay.
  Like that, when Thou ordain'st their Change,
  to thy Command they bend;
  But thou continuest still the same,
  nor have thy Years an End.
28 Thou to the Children of thy Saints
  shall lasting Quiet give;
  Whose happy Race, securely fix'd,
  shall in thy Presence live.

PSALM CIII.

1, 2 MY Soul, inspir'd with sacred Love,
  God's holy Name for ever bless;
  Of all his Favours mindful prove,
  and still thy grateful Thanks express.
3, 4 'Tis He that all thy Sins forgives,
  and after Sickness makes thee sound:
  From Danger he thy Life retrieves,
  by him with Grace and Mercy crown'd.
5, 6 He with good Things thy Mouth supplies,
  thy Vigour, Eagle-like, renews;

He,

PSALM ciii.

He, when the guiltless Suff'rer cries,
   his Foes with just Revenge pursues.
7 God made of old his righteous Ways
   to *Moses* and our Fathers known;
His Works, to his eternal Praise,
   were to the Sons of *Jacob* shown.
8 The Lord abounds with tender Love,
   and unexampled Acts of Grace:
His waken'd Wrath doth slowly move,
   his willing Mercy flies apace.
9, 10 God will not always harshly chide,
   but with his Anger quickly part;
And loves his Punishments to guide
   more by his Love than our Desert.
11 As high as Heav'n its Arch extends
   above this little Spot of Clay;
So much his boundless Love transcends
   the small Respects that we can pay.
12, 13 As far as 'tis from East to West,
   so far hath He our Sins remov'd,
Who with a Father's tender Breast
   hath such as fear'd him always lov'd.
14, 15 For God, who all our Frame surveys,
   considers that we are but Clay;
How fresh soe'er we seem, our Days
   like Grass or Flow'rs must fade away:
16, 17 Whilst they are nipp'd with sudden Blasts,
   nor can we find their former Place;
God's faithful Mercy ever lasts,
   to those that fear Him, and their Race.
18 This shall attend on such as still
   proceed in his appointed Way;
And who not only know his Will,
   but to it just Obedience pay.
19, 20 The Lord, the universal King,
   in Heav'n has fix'd his lofty Throne:
To Him, ye Angels, Praises sing,
   in whose great Strength his Pow'r is shown.
Ye that his just Commands obey,
   and hear and do his sacred Will;
21 Ye Hosts of his this Tribute pay,
   who still what he ordains fulfil.

22 Let ev'ry Creature jointly bless
 the mighty Lord: And thou, my Heart,
With grateful Joy thy Thanks express,
 and in this Concert bear thy Part.

PSALM CIV.

1 BLESS God, my Soul; Thou, Lord, alone
 possessest Empire without Bounds:
With Honour thou art crown'd, thy Throne
 eternal Majesty surrounds.
2 With Light thou dost thyself enrobe,
 and Glory for a Garment take;
Heav'n's Curtains stretch beyond the Globe,
 thy Canopy of State to make.
3 God builds on liquid Air, and forms
 his Palace-Chambers in the Skies;
The Clouds his Chariots are, and Storms
 the swift-wing'd Steeds with which he flies.
4 As bright as Flame, as swift as Wind,
 His Ministers Heaven's Palace fill,
To have their sundry Tasks assign'd,
 all proud to serve their Sov'reign's Will.
5,6 Earth on her Centre fix'd He set,
 her Face with Waters overspread;
Nor proudest Mountains dar'd, as yet,
 to lift above the Waves their Head.
7 But, when thy awful Face appear'd,
 th' insulting Waves dispers'd; they fled,
When once thy Thunder's Voice they heard,
 and by their Haste confess'd their Dread.
8 Thence up by secret Tracks they creep;
 and, gushing from the Mountains Side,
Thro' Vallies travel to the Deep,
 appointed to receive their Tide.
9 There hast thou fix'd the Ocean's Bounds,
 the threat'ning Surges to repel;
That they no more o'erpass their Mounds,
 nor to a second Deluge swell.

PART II.

10 Yet thence in smaller Parties drawn
 the Sea recovers her lost Hills;

And

PSALM civ.

And starting Springs from ev'ry Lawn
supply the Vales with plenteous Rills.
11 The Field's tame Beasts are thither led,
weary with Labour, faint with Drought;
And Asses on wild Mountains bred
have Sense to find these Currents out.
12 There shady Trees from scorching Beams
yield Shelter to the feather'd Throng;
They drink, and to the bounteous Streams
return the Tribute of their Song.
13 His Rains from Heav'n parch'd Hills recruit,
that soon transmit the liquid Store;
Till Earth is burthen'd with her Fruit,
and Nature's Lap can hold no more:
14 Grafs for our Cattle to devour
He makes the Growth of ev'ry Field;
Herbs for Man's Use, of various Pow'r,
that either Food or Physic yield.
15 With cluster'd Grapes He crowns the Vine,
to cheer Man's Heart opprefs'd with Cares;
Gives Oil that makes his Face to shine,
and Corn that wasted Strength repairs.

PART III.

16 The Trees of God, without the Care
or Art of Man, with Sap are fed;
The Mountain Cedar looks as fair,
as those in Royal Gardens bred.
17 Safe in the lofty Cedar's Arms
The Wand'rers of the Air may rest;
The hospitable Pine from Harms
protects the Stork, her pious Guest.
18 Wild Goats the craggy Rock ascend,
its tow'ring Heights their Fortrefs make,
Whose Cells in Labyrinths extend,
where feebler Creatures Refuge take.
19 The Moon's inconstant Aspect shews
th' appointed Seasons of the Year;
Th' instructed Sun his Duty knows,
his Hours to rise and disappear.
20, 21 Darkness He makes the Earth to shroud,
when Forest Beasts securely stray;

Young Lions roar their Wants aloud
  to Providence, that sends them Prey.
22 They range all Night, on Slaughter bent,
  till fummon'd by the rifing Morn,
To fkulk in Dens, with one Confent,
  the confcious Ravagers return.
23 Forth to the Tillage of his Soil
  the Hufbandman fecurely goes,
Commencing with the Sun his Toil,
  with him returns to his Repofe.
24 How various, Lord, thy Works are found:
  for which thy Wifdom we adore!
The Earth is with thy Treafure crown'd,
  'till Nature's Hand can grafp no more.

PART IV.

25 But ftill the vaft unfathom'd Main
  of Wonders a new Scene fupplies,
Whofe Depths Inhabitants contain
  of ev'ry Form and ev'ry Size.
26 Full-freighted Ships from ev'ry Port
  there cut their unmolefted Way;
Leviathan, whom there to fport
  Thou mad'ft, has Compafs there to play.
27 Thefe various Troops of Sea and Land
  in Senfe of common Want agree:
All wait on thy difpenfing Hand,
  and have their daily Alms from Thee.
28 They gather what thy Stores difperfe,
  without their Trouble to provide:
Thou op'ft thy Hand, the Univerfe,
  the craving World, is all fupply'd.
29 Thou for a Moment hid'ft thy Face,
  the num'rous Ranks of Creatures mourn:
Thou tak'ft their Breath, all Nature's Race
  forthwith to Mother Earth return.
30 Again Thou fend'ft thy Spirit forth,
  to infpire the Mafs with vital Seed;
Nature's reftor'd, and Parent Earth
  fmiles on her new-created Breed.
31 Thus through fucceffive Ages ftands
  firm fix'd thy providential Care;

Pleas'd

Pleas'd with the Work of thy own Hands,
    Thou doſt the Waſtes of Time repair.
32 One Look of Thine, one wrathful Look,
    Earth's panting Breaſt with Terror fills;
  One Touch from Thee, with Clouds of Smoke,
    in Darkneſs ſhrouds the proudeſt Hills.
33 In praiſing God while He prolongs
    my Breath, I will that Breath employ;
34 And join Devotion to my Songs.
    ſincere, as in Him is my Joy:
35 While Sinners from Earth's Race are hurl'd,
    my Soul, praiſe thou his holy Name.
  Till with my Song the liſt'ning World
    join Concert, and his Praiſe proclaim.

PSALM CV.

1 O Render Thanks, and bleſs the Lord;
    invoke his ſacred Name;
  Acquaint the Nations with his Deeds,
    his matchleſs Deeds proclaim:
2 Sing to his Praiſe in lofty Hymns,
    his wonderous Works rehearſe;
  Make them the Theme of your Diſcourſe,
    and Subject of your Verſe.
3 Rejoice in his Almighty Name,
    alone to be ador'd;
  And let their Hearts o'erflow with Joy,
    that humbly ſeek the Lord.
4 Seek ye the Lord, his ſaving Strength
    devoutly ſtill implore;
  And where He's ever preſent, ſeek
    his Face for evermore.
5 The Wonders that his Hands have wrought
    keep thankfully in Mind;
  The righteous Statutes of his Mouth,
    and Laws to us aſſign'd;
6 Know ye his Servant *Abr'am's* Seed,
    and *Jacob's* choſen Race.
7 He's ſtill our God, his Judgments ſtill
    throughout the Earth take Place.
8 His Cov'nant He hath kept in Mind
    for num'rous Ages paſt,

Which yet for Thousand Ages more
  in equal Force shall last.
9 First sign'd to *Abra'm*, next by Oath
  to *Isaac* made secure;
10 To *Jacob* and his Heirs a Law
  for ever to endure:
11 That *Canaan's* Land should be their Lot,
  when yet but few they were:
12 But few in Number, and those few
  all friendless Strangers there.
13 In Pilgrimage, from Realm to Realm,
  securely they remov'd:
14 Whilst proudest Monarchs, for their Sakes,
  severely he reprov'd:
15 "These mine Anointed are, said He,
  " Let none my Servants wrong,
  " Nor treat the poorest Prophet ill
  " that does to me belong."
16 A Dearth at last, by his Command,
  did through the Land prevail;
  Till Corn, the chief Support of Life,
  sustaining Corn did fail.
17 But his indulgent Providence
  had pious *Joseph* sent,
  Sold into *Egypt*, but their Death
  who sold him to prevent.
18 His Feet with heavy Chains were crush'd,
  with Calumny his Fame;
19 Till God's appointed Time and Word
  to his Deliv'rance came.
20 The King his Sov'reign Orders sent,
  and rescued him with Speed;
  Whom private Malice had confin'd,
  the People's Ruler freed.
21 His Court, Revenues, Realms, were all
  subjected to his Will;
22 His greatest Princes to controul,
  and teach his Statesmen Skill.

PART II.

23 To *Egypt*, then, invited Guests,
  half-famish'd *Israel* came;

And

And *Jacob* held, by Royal Grant,
  the fertile Soil of *Ham*.
24 Th' Almighty there with such Increase
  his People multiply'd,
  Till with their proud Oppressors they
  in Strength and Numbers vy'd.
25 Their vast Increase th' *Egyptian* Hearts
  with jealous Anger fir'd,
  Till they his Servants to destroy
  by treach'rous Arts confpir'd.
26 His Servant *Moses* then he sent,
  his chosen *Aaron* too;
27 Empower'd with Signs and Miracles
  to prove their Mission true.
28 He call'd for Darkness, Darkness came,
  Nature his Summons knew:
29 Each Stream and Lake, transform'd to Blood,
  the wond'ring Fishes flew.
30 In putrid Floods, throughout the Land,
  the Pest of Frogs was bred;
  From noisome Fens sent up to croak
  at *Pharaoh's* Board and Bed.
31 He gave the Sign, and Swarms of Flies
  came down in cloudy Hosts,
  Whilst Earth's enliven'd Dust below
  bred Lice thro' all their Coasts.
32 He sent them batt'ring Hail for Rain,
  and Fire for cooling Dew;
33 He smote their Vines and Forest Plants,
  and Gardens' Pride o'erthrew.
34 He spake the Word, and Locusts came
  with Caterpillars join'd;
  They prey'd upon the poor Remains
  the Storm had left behind.
35 From Trees to Herbage they descend,
  no verdant Thing they spare;
  But, like the naked fallow Field,
  leave all the Pastures bare.
36 From Fields to Villages and Towns
  commission'd Vengeance flew:
  One fatal Stroke their eldest Hopes
  and Strength of *Egypt* slew.

37 He brought his Servants forth, enrich'd
  with *Egypt's* borrow'd Wealth;
And, what tranfcends all Treafure elfe,
  enrich'd with vig'rous Health.
38 *Egypt* rejoic'd, in Hopes to find
  her Plagues with them remov'd;
Taught dearly now to fear worfe Ills
  by thofe already prov'd.
39 Their fhrouding Canopy by Day
  a journeying Cloud was fpread;
A fiery Pillar all the Night
  their Defert-Marches led.
40 They long'd for Flefh; with Ev'ning Quails
  He furnifh'd ev'ry Tent;
From Heaven's own Granary, each Morn
  the Bread of Angels fent.
41 He fmote the Rock, whofe flinty Breaft
  pour'd forth a gufhing Tide;
Whofe flowing Streams, where'er they march'd,
  the Defert's Drought fupply'd.
42 For ftill He did on *Abra'm's* Faith
  an ancient League reflect:
43 He brought his People forth with Joy,
  with Triumph his Elect.
44 Quite rooting out their Heathen Foes
  from *Canaan's* fertile Soil,
To them in cheap Poffeffion gave
  the Fruit of others' Toil:
45 That they his Statutes might obferve,
  his facred Laws obey.
For Benefits fo vaft, let us
  our Songs of Praife repay.

PSALM CVI.

1 O Render Thanks to God above,
    The Fountain of eternal Love;
  Whofe Mercy firm through Ages paft
  Has ftood, and fhall for ever laft.
2 Who can his mighty Deeds exprefs,
  Not only vaft, but numberlefs?
  What mortal Eloquence can raife
  His Tribute to immortal Praife?

PSALM cvi.

3 Happy are they, and only they,
   Who from thy Judgments never ſtray:
   Who know what's right; not only ſo,
   But always practiſe what they know.
4 Extend to me that Favour, Lord,
   Thou to thy Choſen doſt afford;
   When Thou return'ſt to ſet them free,
   Let thy Salvation viſit me.
5 O may I worthy prove to ſee
   Thy Saints in full Proſperity;
   That I the joyful Choir may join,
   And count thy People's Triumph mine.
6 But, ah! can we expect ſuch Grace,
   Of Parents vile the viler Race;
   Who their Miſdeeds have acted o'er,
   And with new Crimes increas'd the Score?
7 Ingrateful, they no longer thought
   On all his Works in *Egypt* wrought;
   The Red Sea they no ſooner view'd,
   But they their baſe Diſtruſt renew'd.
8 Yet He, to vindicate his Name,
   Once more to their Deliv'rance came,
   To make his ſov'reign Pow'r be known,
   That He is God, and He alone.
9 To Right and Left, at his Command,
   The parting Deep diſclos'd her Sand;
   Where firm and dry the Paſſage lay
   As through ſome parch'd and deſert Way.
10 Thus reſcu'd from their Foes they were,
    Who cloſely preſs'd upon their Rear:
11 Whoſe Rage purſued them to thoſe Waves,
    That prov'd the raſh Purſuers' Graves.
12 The wat'ry Mountains ſudden Fall
    O'erwhelm'd proud *Pharaoh*, Hoſt and all.
    This Proof did ſtupid *Iſrael* move
    To own God's Truth, and praiſe his Love.

PART II.

13 But ſoon theſe Wonders they forgot,
    And for his Counſel waited not:
14 But, luſting in the Wilderneſs,
    Did Him with freſh Temptations preſs.

15 Strong Food at their Requeſt He ſent,
But made their Sin their Puniſhment.
16 Yet ſtill his Saints they did oppoſe,
The Prieſt and Prophet whom he choſe.
17 But Earth, the Quarrel to decide,
Her vengeful Jaws extended wide;
Raſh *Dathan* to her Centre drew,
With proud *Abiram's* factious Crew.
18 The reſt of thoſe who did conſpire
To kindle wild Sedition's Fire,
With all their impious Train, became
A Prey to Heaven's devouring Flame.
19 Near *Horeb's* Mount a Calf they made,
And to the molten Image pray'd;
20 Adoring what their Hands did frame,
They chang'd their Glory to their Shame,
21 Their God and Saviour they forgot,
And all his Works in *Egypt* wrought;
22 His Signs in *Ham's* aſtoniſh'd Coaſt,
And where proud *Pharoah's* Troops were loſt,
23 Thus urg'd, his vengeful Hand he rear'd,
But *Moſes* in the Breach appear'd;
The Saint did for the Rebels pray,
And turn'd Heaven's kindled Wrath away.
24, 25 Yet they his pleaſant Land deſpis'd,
Nor his repeated Promiſe priz'd;
Nor did th' Almighty's Voice obey;
But when God ſaid, *Go up*, would ſtay.
26, 27 This ſeal'd their Doom, without Redreſs,
To periſh in the Wilderneſs;
Or elſe to be by Heathens Hands
O'erthrown, and ſcatter'd through the Lands.

PART III.

28 Yet, unreclaim'd, this ſtubborn Race
Baal Peor's Worſhip did embrace;
Became his impious Gueſts, and fed
On Sacrifices to the Dead.
29 Thus they perſiſted to provoke
God's Vengeance to the final Stroke.
'Tis come:—the deadly Peſt is come
To execute their gen'ral Doom.

30, But

PSALM cvi.

30 But *Phineas*, fir'd with holy Rage,
(Th' Almighty's Vengeance to affuage)
Did, by two bold Offenders Fall,
Th' Atonement make that ranfom'd All.

31 As him a heavenly Zeal had mov'd,
So Heaven the zealous Act approv'd;
To him confirming, and his Race,
The Prieſthood he fo well did grace.

32 At *Meribah* God's Wrath they mov'd,
Who *Mofes* for their Sakes reprov'd;

33 Whofe patient Soul they did provoke,
Till raſhly the meek Prophet fpoke.

34 Nor, when poffefs'd of *Canaan's* Land,
Did they perform their Lord's Command;
Nor his commiffion'd Sword employ
The guilty Nations to deſtroy.

35 Not only fpar'd the Pagan Crew,
But, mingling, learnt their Vices too;

36. And Worſhip to thofe Idols paid,
Which them to fatal Snares betray'd.

37, 38 To Devils they did facrifice
Their Children with relentlefs Eyes;
Approach'd their Altars thro' a Flood
Of their own Sons and Daughters Blood.
No cheaper Victims would appeafe
Canaan's remorfelefs Deities;
No Blood her Idols reconcile,
But that which did the Land defile.

PART IV.

39 Nor did thefe favage Cruelties
The harden'd Reprobates fuffice;
For after their Hearts Lufts they went,
And daily did new Crimes invent.

40 But Sins of fuch infernal Hue
God's Wrath againſt his People drew,
Till He, their once indulgent Lord,
His own Inheritance abhorr'd.

41 He them defencelefs did expofe
To their infulting Heathen Foes;
And made them on the Triumphs wait
Of thofe who bore them greateſt Hate.

42 Nor

42 Nor thus his Indignation ceas'd;
   Their List of Tyrants He increas'd,
   Till they, who God's mild Sway declin'd,
   Were made the Vassals of Mankind.
43 Yet, when distress'd they did repent,
   His Anger did as oft relent:
   But freed, they did his Wrath provoke,
   Renew'd their Sins, and He their Yoke.
44 Nor yet implacable He prov'd,
   Nor heard their wretched Cries unmov'd;
45 But did to Mind his Promise bring,
   And Mercy's inexausted Spring.
46 Compassion too he did impart,
   Ev'n to their Foes obdurate Heart,
   And Pity for their Suff'rings bred
   In those who them to Bondage led.
47 Still save us, Lord, and *Israel's* Bands
   Together bring from Heathen Lands;
   So to thy Name our Thanks we'll raise,
   And ever triumph in thy Praise.
48 Let *Israel's* God be ever bless'd,
   His Name eternally confess'd:
   Let all his Saints with full Accord
   Sing loud *Amens*——Praise ye the Lord.

PSALM CVII.

1 TO God your grateful Voices raise,
      Who does your daily Patron prove:
   And let your never-ceasing Praise
      Attend on his eternal Love.
2,3 Let those give Thanks whom He from Bands
      Of proud oppressing Foes releas'd:
   And brought them back from distant Lands,
      From North and South, and West and East.
4,5 Through lonely desert Ways they went,
      Nor could a peopled City find:
   Till, quite with Thirst and Hunger spent,
      Their fainting Souls within them pin'd.
6 Then soon to God's indulgent Ear
      Did they their mournful Cry address;
   Who graciously vouchsaf'd to hear,
      And freed them from their deep Distress.

7 From crooked Paths he led them forth,
  And in the certain Way did guide
 To wealthy Towns of great Resort,
  Where all their Wants were well supply'd.
8 O then that all the Earth with me
  Would God for this his Goodness praise!
 And for the mighty Works which He
  Throughout the wondring World displays!
9 For He, from Heav'n, the sad Estate
  Of longing Souls with Pity views;
 To hungry Souls that pant for Meat,
  His Goodness daily Food renews.

PART II.

10 Some lie, with Darkness compass'd round,
   In Death's uncomfortable Shade;
  And with unweildy Fetters bound,
   By pressing Cares more heavy made.
11,12 Because God's Counsel they defy'd,
   And lightly priz'd his holy Word,
  With these Afflictions they were try'd:
   They fell, and none could Help afford.
13 Then soon to God's indulgent Ear,
   Did they their mournful Cry address;
  Who graciously vouchsaf'd to hear,
   And freed them from their deep Distress.
14 From dismal Dungeons, dark as Night,
   And Shades as black as Death's Abode,
  He brought them forth to cheerful Light,
   And welcome Liberty bestow'd.
15 O then that all the Earth with me
   Would God for this his Goodness praise;
  And for the mighty Works which He
   Throughout the wond'ring World displays!
16 For He, with his Almighty Hand,
   The Gates of Brass in Pieces broke;
  Nor could the massy Bars withstand,
   Or temper'd Steel resist the Stroke.

PART III.

17 Remorseless Wretches, void of Sense,
   With bold Transgressions God defy;

And,

And, for their multiply'd Offence,
Oppress'd with sore Diseases lie:
18 Their Soul, a Prey to Pain and Fear,
Abhors to take the choicest Meats;
And they by faint Degrees draw near
To Death's inhospitable Gates.
19 Then straight to God's indulgent Ear
Do they their mournful Cry address;
Who graciously vouchsafes to hear,
And frees them from their deep Distress.
20 He all their sad Distempers heals,
His Word both Health and Safety gives;
And, when all human Succour fails,
From near Destruction them retrieves.
21 O then that all the Earth with me
Would God for this his Goodness praise!
And for the mighty Works which He
Throughout the wond'ring World displays!
22 With Off'rings let his Altar flame,
Whilst they their grateful Thanks express,
And with loud Joy his holy Name
For all his Acts of Wonder bless!

PART IV.

23, 24 They that in Ships with Courage bold
O'er swelling Waves their Trade pursue,
Do God's amazing Works behold,
And in the Deep his Wonders view.
25 No sooner his Command is past,
But forth a dreadful Tempest flies,
Which sweeps the Sea with rapid Haste,
And makes the stormy Billows rise.
26 Sometimes the Ships, toss'd up to Heav'n,
On Tops of Mountain Waves appear;
Then down the steep Abyss are driv'n,
Whilst ev'ry Soul dissolves with Fear.
27 They reel and stagger to and fro,
Like Men with Fumes of Wine oppress'd:
Nor do the skilful Seamen know
Which Way to steer, what Course is best.
28 Then straight to God's indulgent Ear
They do their mournful Cry address;

Who

PSALM cvii.

Who graciously vouchsafes to hear,
    And frees them from their deep Distress.
29, 30 He does the raging Storm appease,
    And makes the Billows calm and still;
With Joy they see their Fury cease,
    And their intended Course fulfil.
31 O then that all the Earth with me
    Would God for this his Goodness praise!
And for the mighty Works which He
    Throughout the wond'ring World displays!
32 Let them, where all the Tribes resort,
    Advance to Heav'n his glorious Name,
And in the Elders sov'reign Court
    With one Consent his Praise proclaim!

PART V.

33, 34 A fruitful Land, where Streams abound,
    God's just Revenge, if People sin,
Will turn to dry and barren Ground,
    To punish those that dwell therein.
35, 36 The parch'd and desert Heath he makes
    To flow with Streams and springing Wells;
Which for his Lot the Hungry takes,
    And in strong Cities safely dwells.
37, 38 He sows the Field, the Vineyard plants,
    Which gratefully his Toil repay;
Nor can, whilst God his Blessing grants,
    His fruitful Seed or Stock decay.
39 But, when his Sins Heaven's Wrath provoke,
    His Health and Substance fade away;
He feels th' Oppressor's galling Yoke,
    And is of Grief the wretched Prey.
40 The Prince, that slights what God commands,
    Expos'd to Scorn must quit his Throne;
And over wild and desert Lands,
    Where no Path offers, stray alone.
41 Whilst God from all afflicting Cares
    Sets up the humble Man on high;
And makes in Time his num'rous Heirs
    With his increasing Flocks to vie.
42, 43 Then Sinners shall have nought to say,
    The Just a decent Joy shall show:

The Wise these strange Events shall weigh,
And thence God's Goodness fully know.

PSALM CVIII.

1 O GOD, my Heart is fully bent
    to magnify thy Name;
  My Tongue with cheerful Songs of Praise
    shall celebrate thy Fame.
2 Awake, my Lute; nor thou, my Harp,
    thy warbling Notes delay;
  Whilst I with early Hymns of Joy
    prevent the dawning Day.
3 To all the list'ning Tribes, O Lord,
    thy Wonders I will tell,
  And to those Nations sing thy Praise
    that round about us dwell:
4 Because thy Mercy's boundless Height
    the highest Heav'n transcends,
  And far beyond th' aspiring Clouds
    Thy faithful Truth extends.
5 Be Thou, O God, exalted high
    above the starry Frame;
  And let the World, with one Consent,
    confess thy glorious Name.
6 That all thy chosen People Thee
    their Saviour may declare;
  Let thy Right-hand protect me still,
    and answer thou my Pray'r.
7 Since God himself has said the Word,
    whose Promise cannot fail,
  With Joy I *Sichem* will divide,
    and measure *Succoth's* Vale;
8 *Gi'ead* is mine, *Manasseh* too,
    and *Ephraim* owns my Cause:
  Their Strength my Regal Pow'r supports,
    and *Judah* gives my Laws.
9 *Moab* I'll make my servile Drudge,
    on vanquish'd *Edom* tread:
  And thro' the proud *Philistine* Lands
    my conqu'ring Banners spread.
10 By whose Support and Aid shall I
    their well-fenc'd City gain?

Who

PSALM cviii, cix.

Who will my Troops securely lead
  thro' *Edom's* guarded Plain?
11 Lord, wilt not Thou assist our Arms,
  which late Thou didst forsake?
And wilt not Thou, of these our Hosts,
  once more the Guidance take?
12 O to thy Servants in Distress
  thy speedy Succour send;
For vain it is on human Aid
  for Safety to depend.
13 Then valiant Acts shall we perform,
  if Thou thy Pow'r disclose;
For God it is, and God alone,
  that treads down all our Foes.

PSALM CIX.

1 O GOD, whose former Mercies make
    my constant Praise thy Due,
  Hold not thy Peace, but my sad State
    with wonted Favour view.
2 For sinful Men, with lying Lips,
    deceitful Speeches frame,
  And with their study'd Slanders seek
    to wound my spotless Fame.
3 Their restless Hatred prompts them still
    malicious Lies to spread;
  And all against my Life combine,
    by causeless Fury led.
4 Those, whom with tend'rest Love I us'd,
    my chief Opposers are;
  Whilst I, of other Friends bereft,
    resort to Thee by Pray'r.
5 Since Mischief, for the Good I did,
    their strange Reward does prove;
  And Hatred's the Return they make
    for undissembled Love:
6 Their guilty Leader shall be made
    to some ill Man a Slave;
  And when he's try'd, his mortal Foe
    for his Accuser have.
7 His Guilt, when Sentence is pronounc'd,
    shall meet a dreadful Fate,

L 2   Whilst

Whilst his rejected Pray'r but serves
   his Crimes to aggravate.
8 He, snatch'd by some untimely Fate,
   shan't live out half his Days:
   Another, by Divine Decree,
   shall on his Office seize.
9, 10 His Seed shall Orphans be, his Wife
   a Widow plung'd in Grief;
   His vagrant Children beg their Bread,
   where none can give Relief.
11 His ill-got Riches shall be made
   to Usurers a Prey;
   The Fruit of all his Toil shall be
   by Strangers borne away.
12 None shall be found that to his Wants
   their Mercy will extend,
   Or to his helpless Orphan Seed
   the least Assistance lend.
13 A swift Destruction soon shall seize
   on his unhappy Race;
   And the next Age his hated Name
   shall utterly deface.
14 The Vengeance of his Father's Sins
   upon his Head shall fall;
   God on his Mother's Crimes shall think,
   and punish him for all.
15 All these in horrid Order rank'd
   before the Lord shall stand,
   Till his fierce Anger quite cuts off
   their Mem'ry from the Land.

PART II.

16 Because he never Mercy shew'd,
   but still the Poor oppress'd;
   And sought to slay the helpless Man,
   with heavy Woes distress'd:
17 Therefore the Curse he lov'd to vent
   shall his own Portion prove;
   And Blessing, which he still abhorr'd,
   shall far from him remove.
18 Since he in Cursing took such Pride,
   like Water it shall spread

Thro'

PSALM cix.

Thro' all his Veins, and stick like Oil
   with which his Bones are fed.
19 This, like a poison'd Robe, shall still
   his constant Cov'ring be;
Or an envenom'd Belt, from which
   he never shall be free.
20 Thus shall the Lord reward all those
   that Ill to me design;
That with malicious false Reports
   against my Life combine.
21 But, for thy glorious Name, O God,
   do Thou deliver me;
And, for thy plenteous Mercy's Sake,
   preserve and set me free:
22 For I, to utmost Straits reduc'd,
   am void of all Relief:
My Heart is wounded with Distress,
   and quite pierc'd thro' with Grief.
23 I, like an Ev'ning Shade, decline,
   which vanishes apace:
Like Locusts up and down I'm toss'd,
   and have no certain Place.
24, 25 My Knees with fasting are grown weak,
   my Body lank and lean;
All that behold me shake their Heads,
   and treat me with Disdain.
26, 27 But, for thy Mercy's Sake, O Lord,
   do Thou my Foes withstand;
That all may see 'tis thy own Act,
   the Work of thy Right-hand.
28 Then let them curse, so thou but bless;
   let Shame the Portion be
Of all that my Destruction seek,
   while I rejoice in Thee.
29 My Foe shall with Disgrace be cloath'd,
   and, spite of all his Pride,
His own Confusion, like a Cloak,
   the guilty Wretch shall hide.
30 But I to God, in grateful Thanks,
   my cheerful Voice will raise;
And, where the great Assembly meets,
   set forth his noble Praise.

31 For Him the Poor shall always find
  their sure and constant Friend;
  And He shall from unrighteous Dooms
  their guiltless Souls defend.

PSALM CX.

1 THE Lord unto my Lord thus spake,
  " Till I thy Foes thy Footstool make,
  " Sit thou in State, at my Right-hand:
2 " Supreme in *Sion* thou shall be,
  " And all thy proud Opposers see
  " Subjected to thy just Command.
3 " Thee in thy Power's triumphant Day
  " The willing Nations shall obey;
  " And, when thy rising Beams they view,
  " Shall all (redeem'd from Error's Night)
  " Appear as numberless and bright
  " As Chrystal Drops of Morning Dew."
4 The Lord hath sworn, nor sworn in vain,
  That, like *Melchisedech's*, thy Reign
  And Priesthood shall no Period know;
5 No proud Competitor to sit
  At thy Right-hand will He permit,
  But in his Wrath crown'd Heads o'erthrow.
6 The sentenc'd Heathen He shall slay,
  And fill with Carcases his Way,
  Till he hath struck Earth's Tyrants dead;
7 But in the Highway Brooks shall first,
  Like a poor Pilgrim, slake his Thirst,
  And then in Triumph raise his Head.

PSALM CXI.

1 PRAISE ye the Lord; our God to praise
  My Soul her utmost Pow'rs shall raise;
  With private Friends, and in the Throng
  Of Saints, his Praise shall be my Song.
2 His Works, for Greatness tho' renown'd,
  His wondrous Works with Ease are found
  By those who seek for them aright,
  And in the pious Search delight.
3 His Works are all of matchless Fame,
  And universal Glory claim;

His Truth, confirm'd thro' Ages paſt,
Shall to eternal Ages laſt.
4 By Precepts He has us enjoin'd
To keep his wondrous Works in Mind;
And to Poſterity record
That good and gracious is our Lord.
5 His Bounty, like a flowing Tide,
Has all his Servants' Wants ſupply'd;
And he will ever keep in Mind
His Cov'nant with our Fathers ſign'd.
6 At once, aſtoniſh'd and o'erjoy'd,
They ſaw his matchleſs Pow'r employ'd;
Whereby the Heathen were ſuppreſs'd,
And we their Heritage poſſeſs'd.
7 Juſt are the Dealings of his Hands,
Immutable are his Commands:
8 By Truth and Equity ſuſtain'd,
And for eternal Rules ordain'd,
9 He ſet his Saints from Bondage free,
And then eſtabliſh'd his Decree,
For ever to remain the ſame;
Holy and reverend is his Name.
10 Who Wiſdom's ſacred Prize would win,
Muſt with the Fear of God begin;
Immortal Praiſe and heavenly Skill
Have they who know and do his Will.

PSALM CXII.
HALLELUJAH.

1 THAT Man is bleſt who ſtands in Awe
Of God, and loves his ſacred Law:
2 His Seed on Earth ſhall be renown'd,
And with ſucceſſive Honours crown'd.
3 His Houſe, the Seat of Wealth, ſhall be
An inexhauſted Treaſury;
His Juſtice, free from all Decay,
Shall Bleſſings to his Heirs convey.
4 The Soul that's fill'd with Virtue's Light
Shines brighteſt in Affliction's Night;
To pity the Diſtreſs'd inclin'd,
As well as juſt to all Mankind.

5 His lib'ral Favours he extends;
To some he gives, to others lends;
Yet what his Charity impairs
He saves by Prudence in Affairs.

6 Beset with threat'ning Dangers round,
Unmov'd shall he maintain his Ground;
The sweet Remembrance of the Just
Shall flourish when he sleeps in Dust.

7 Ill Tidings never can surprize
His Heart that, fix'd, on God relies;

8 On Safety's Rock he sits, and sees
The Shipwreck of his Enemies.

9 His Hands, while they his Alms bestow'd,
His Glory's future Harvest sow'd;
Whence he shall reap Wealth, Fame, Renown,
A temporal and eternal Crown.

10 The Wicked shall his Triumph see,
And gnash their Teeth in Agony;
While their unrighteous Hopes decay,
And vanish with themselves away.

PSALM CXIII.

1 YE Saints and Servants of the Lord,
    The Triumphs of his Name record;
2   His sacred Name for ever bless.
3 Where-e'er the circling Sun displays
His rising Beams or setting Rays,
    Due Praise to his great Name address.

4 God thro' the World extends his Sway;
The Regions of eternal Day
    But Shadows of his Glory are.

5 With Him, whose Majesty excels,
Who made the Heaven in which He dwells,
    Let no created Power compare.

6 Tho' 'tis beneath his State to view
In highest Heaven what Angels do,
    Yet He to Earth vouchsafes his Care;
He takes the Needy from his Cell,
Advancing him in Courts to dwell,
    Companion to the greatest there.

7 When childless Families despair,
He sends the Blessing of an Heir,
    To rescue their expiring Name;

Makes

Makes her that barren was to bear,
  And joyfully her Fruit to rear.
  O then extol his matchless Fame!

PSALM CXIV.

1 WHEN *Israel*, by th' Almighty led,
    (enrich'd with their Oppressors' Spoil)
  From *Egypt* march'd; and *Jacob's* Seed
    from Bondage in a foreign Soil;
2 *Jehovah*, for his Residence,
    chose out Imperial *Judah's* Tent,
  His Mansion royal, and from thence
    thro' *Israel's* Camp his Orders sent.
3 The distant Sea with Terror saw,
    and from th' Almighty's Presence fled;
  Old *Jordan's* Streams, surpriz'd with Awe,
    retreated to their Fountain's Head.
4 The taller Mountains skipp'd like Rams,
    when Danger near the Fold they hear;
  The Hills skipp'd after them like Lambs,
    affrighted by their Leader's Fear.
5 O Sea, what made your Tide withdraw,
    and naked leave your oozy Bed?
  Why, *Jordan*, against Nature's Law,
    recoil'd thou to thy Fountain's Head?
6 Why, Mountains, did ye skip like Rams,
    when Danger does approach the Fold?
  Why after you the Hills like Lambs,
    when they their Leader's Flight behold?
7 Earth, tremble on; well may'st thou fear
    thy Lord and Maker's Face to see:
  When *Jacob's* awful God draws near,
    'tis Time for Earth and Sea to flee.
8 To flee from God, who Nature's Law
    confirms and cancels at his Will;
  Who Springs from flinty Rocks can draw,
    and thirsty Vales with Water fill.

PSALM CXV.

1 LORD, not to us, we claim no Share,
    but to thy sacred Name
  Give Glory for thy Mercy's Sake,
    and Truth's eternal Fame.

PSALM cxv.

2 Why should the Heathen cry, Where's now
  the God whom we adore?
3 Convince them that in Heav'n Thou art,
  and uncontrol'd thy Pow'r.
4 Their Gods but Gold and Silver are,
  the Works of mortal Hands;
5 With speechless Mouth and sightless Eyes
  the molten Image stands.
6 The Pageant hath both Ears and Nose,
  but neither hears nor smells;
7 Its Hands and Feet nor feel nor move;
  no Life within it dwells.
8 Such senseless Stocks they are, that we
  can nothing like them find,
  But those who on their Help rely,
  and them for Gods design'd.
9 O, *Israel*, make the Lord your Trust,
  who is your Help and Shield;
10 Priests, Levites, trust in Him alone,
  who only Help can yield.
11 Let all, who truly fear the Lord,
  on Him they fear rely;
  Who them in Danger can defend,
  and all their Wants supply.
12, 13 Of us He oft has mindful been,
  and *Israel's* House will bless;
  Priests, Levites, Proselytes, e'en all
  who his great Name confess.
14 On you, and on your Heirs, He will
  Increase of Blessings bring:
15 Thrice happy you, who Fav'rites are
  of this Almighty King.
16 Heaven's highest Orb of Glory He
  his Empire's Seat design'd;
  And gave this lower Globe of Earth
  a Portion to Mankind.
17 They, who in Death and Silence sleep,
  to Him no Praise afford;
18 But we will bless for evermore
  our ever-living Lord.

PSALM

PSALM CXVI.

1 MY Soul with grateful Thoughts of Love
entirely is poffeft,
Becaufe the Lord vouchfaf'd to hear
the Voice of my Requeft.
2 Since He has now his Ear inclin'd,
I never will defpair;
But ftill in all the Straits of Life
to Him addrefs my Pray'r.
3 With deadly Sorrows compafs'd round;
with Pains of Hell opprefs'd;
When Troubles feiz'd my aching Heart
and Anguifh rack'd my Breaft;
4 On God's Almighty Name I call'd,
and thus to Him I pray'd;
" Lord, I befeech Thee, fave my Soul,
" with Sorrows quite difmay'd."
5, 6 How juft and merciful is God!
how gracious is the Lord!
Who faves the Harmlefs, and to me
does timely Help afford.
7 Then, free from penfive Cares, my Soul,
refume thy wonted Reft;
For God has wondroufly to thee
his bounteous Love expreft.
8 When Death alarm'd me, He remov'd
my Dangers and my Fears:
My Feet from falling he fecur'd,
and dry'd my Eyes from Tears.
9 Therefore my Life's remaining Years,
which God to me fhall lend,
Will I in Praifes to his Name
and in his Service fpend.
10, 11 In God I trufted, and of Him
in greateft Straits did boaft;
(For in my Flight all Hopes of Aid
from faithlefs Men were loft:)
12, 13 Then what Return to Him fhall I
for all his Goodnefs make?
I'll praife his Name, and with glad Zeal
the Cup of Bleffing take.

14, 15 I'll

14, 15 I'll pay my Vows amongst his Saints,
whose Blood (howe'er despis'd
By wicked Men) in God's Account
is always highly priz'd:
16 By various Ties, O Lord, must I
to thy Dominion bow;
Thy humble Handmaid's Son before,
thy ransom'd Captive now;
17, 18 To Thee I'll Off'rings bring of Praise;
and, whilst I bless thy Name,
The just Performance of my Vows
to all thy Saints proclaim.
19 They in *Jerusalem* shall meet,
and in thy House shall join
To bless thy Name with one Consent,
and mix their Songs with mine.

PSALM CXVII.

1 WITH cheerful Notes let all the Earth
to Heav'n their Voices raise:
Let all, inspir'd with godly Mirth,
sing solemn Hymns of Praise.
2 God's tender Mercy knows no Bound,
his Truth shall ne'er decay:
Then let the willing Nations round
their grateful Tribute pay.

PSALM CXVIII.

1, 2 O Praise the Lord, for He is good,
his Mercies ne'er decay:
That his kind Favours ever last,
let thankful *Israel* say.
3, 4 Their Sense of his eternal Love
let *Aaron's* House express;
And, that it never fails, let all
that fear the Lord confess.
5 To God I made my humble Moan,
with Troubles quite opprest:
And he releas'd me from my Straits,
and granted my Request.
6 Since, therefore, God does on my Side
so graciously appear,

Why

PSALM cxviii.

Why should the vain Attemps of Men
  possess my Soul with Fear?
7 Since God with those that aid my Cause
  vouchsafes my Part to take,
To all my Foes I need not doubt
  a just Return to make.
8, 9 For better 'tis to trust in God,
  and have the Lord our Friend,
Than on the greatest human Power
  for Safety to depend.
10, 11 Tho' many Nations, closely leagu'd,
  did oft beset me round;
Yet, by his boundless Power sustain'd,
  I did their Strength confound.
12 They swarm'd like Bees, and yet their Rage
  was but a short-liv'd Blaze;
For whilst on God I still rely'd,
  I vanquish'd them with Ease.
13 When all united press'd me hard,
  in Hopes to make me fall;
The Lord vouchsaf'd to take my Part,
  and sav'd me from them all.
14 The Honour of my strange Escape
  to Him alone belongs;
He is my Saviour and my Strength,
  He only claims my Songs.
15 Joy fills the Dwelling of the Just,
  whom God has sav'd from Harm:
For wond'rous Things are brought to pass
  by his Almighty Arm.
16 He, by his own resistless Power,
  has endless Honour won;
The saving Strength of his Right-Hand
  amazing Works has done.
17 God will not suffer me to fall,
  but still prolongs my Days;
That, by declaring all his Works,
  I may advance his Praise.
18 When God had sorely me chastis'd,
  till quite of Hopes bereav'd,
His Mercy from the Gates of Death
  my fainting Life repriev'd.

19 Then

19 Then open wide the Temple Gates,
  to which the Just repair,
That I may enter in, and praise
  my great Deliv'rer there.
20, 21 Within those Gates of God's Abode,
  to which the Righteous press,
Since Thou hast heard, and set me safe,
  thy holy Name I'll bless.
22, 23 That, which the Builders once refus'd,
  is now the Corner-Stone;
This is the wondrous Work of God,
  the Work of God alone.
24, 25 This Day is God's; let all the Land
  exalt their cheerful Voice:
Lord, we beseech Thee, save us now,
  and make us still rejoice.
26 Him that approaches in God's Name
  let all th' Assembly bless:
" We that belong to God's own House
" have wish'd you good Success."
27 God is the Lord, through whom we all
  both Light and Comfort find:
Fast to the Altar's Horns with Cords
  the chosen Victim bind.
28 Thou art my Lord, O God, and still
  I'll praise thy holy Name;
Because Thou only art my God,
  I'll celebrate thy Fame.
29 O then with me give Thanks to God,
  who still does gracious prove;
And let the Tribute of our Praise
  be endless as his Love.

PSALM CXIX.

ALEPH.

1 HOW bless'd are they who always keep
  the pure and perfect Way;
Who never from the sacred Paths
  of God's Commandments stray!
2 Thrice bless'd, who to his righteous Laws
  have still obedient been!

And

PSALM cxix.

And have with fervent humble Zeal
   his Favour fought to win!
3 Such Men their utmost Caution use
   to shun each wicked Deed;
But in the Path which He directs
   with constant Care proceed.
4 Thou strictly hast enjoin'd us, Lord,
   to learn thy sacred Will;
And all our Diligence employ
   thy Statutes to fulfil.
5 Oh then that thy most holy Will
   might o'er my Ways preside!
And I the Course of all my Life
   by thy Direction guide!
6 Then with Assurance should I walk,
   from all Confusion free;
Convinc'd, with Joy, that all my Ways
   with thy Commands agree.
7 My upright Heart shall my glad Mouth
   with cheerful Praises fill;
When, by thy righteous Judgments taught,
   I shall have learnt thy Will.
8 So to thy sacred Laws shall I
   all due Observance pay:
O then forsake me not, my God,
   nor cast me quite away.

BETH.

9 How shall the Young preserve their Ways
   from all Pollution free?
By making still their Course of Life
   with thy Commands agree.
10 With hearty Zeal for Thee I seek,
   to Thee for Succour pray;
O suffer not my careless Steps
   from thy right Paths to stray.
11 Safe in my Heart, and closely hid,
   thy Word, my Treasure, lies:
To succour me with timely Aid,
   when sinful Thoughts arise.
12 Secur'd by that, my grateful Soul
   shall ever bless thy Name:

O teach

O teach me then by thy just Laws
  my future Life to frame.
13 My Lips, unlock'd by pious Zeal,
  to others have declar'd,
How well the Judgments of thy Mouth
  deserve our best Regard.
14 Whilst in the Way of thy Commands
  more solid Joy I found,
Than had I been with vast Increase
  of envy'd Riches crown'd.
15 Therefore thy just and upright Laws
  shall always fill my Mind,
And those sound Rules, which thou prescrib'st,
  all due Respect shall find.
16 To keep thy Statutes undefac'd,
  shall be my constant Joy;
The strict Remembrance of thy Word
  shall all my Thoughts employ.

GIMEL.

17 Be gracious to thy Servant, Lord;
  do thou my Life defend:
That I, according to thy Word,
  my Time to come may spend.
18 Enlighten both my Eyes and Mind,
  that so I may discern
The wonderous Things which they behold
  who thy just Precepts learn.
19 Tho' like a Stranger in the Land,
  from Place to Place I stray,
Thy righteous Judgments from my Sight
  remove not Thou away.
20 My fainting Soul is almost pin'd,
  with earnest Longing spent;
Whilst always on the eager Search
  of thy just Will intent.
21 Thy sharp Rebuke shall crush the Proud,
  whom still thy Curse pursues;
Since they to walk in thy right Ways
  presumptuously refuse.
22 But far from me do Thou, O Lord,
  Contempt and Shame remove;

For I thy sacred Laws affect
with undissembled Love.
23 Tho' Princes oft, in Council met,
against thy Servant spake;
Yet I thy Statutes to observe
my constant Bus'ness make.
24 For thy Commands have always been
my Comfort and Delight;
By them I learn, with prudent Care,
to guide my Steps aright.

DALETH.

25 My Soul, oppress'd with deadly Care,
close to the Dust does cleave;
Revive me, Lord, and let me now
thy promis'd Aid receive.
26 To Thee I still declar'd my Ways,
and thou inclin'dst thine Ear;
O teach me then my future Life
by thy just Laws to steer.
27 If thou wilt make me know thy Laws,
and by their Guidance walk,
The wondrous Works which thou hast done
shall be my constant Talk.
28 But see, my Soul within me sinks,
press'd down with weighty Care;
Do thou, according to thy Word,
my wasted Strength repair.
29 Far, far from me, be all false Ways
and lying Arts remov'd:
But kindly grant I still may keep
the Path by Thee approv'd.
30 Thy faithful Ways, thou God of Truth,
my happy Choice I've made;
Thy Judgments as my Rule of Life
before me always laid.
31 My Care has been to make my Life
with thy Commands agree;
O then preserve thy Servant, Lord,
from Shame and Ruin free.
32 So in the Way of thy Commands
shall I with Pleasure run,

M And

And with an Heart enlarg'd with Joy
succesfully go on.

H E.

33 Instruct me in thy Statutes, Lord,
thy righteous Paths display;
And I from them, through all my Life,
will never go astray.

34 If Thou true Wisdom from above
wilt graciously impart,
To keep thy perfect Laws I will
devote my zealous Heart.

35 Direct me in the sacred Way
to which thy Precepts lead;
Because my chief Delight has been
thy righteous Paths to tread.

36 Do Thou to thy most just Commands
incline my willing Heart;
Let no Desire of worldly Wealth
from Thee my Thoughts divert.

37 From those vain Objects turn my Eyes,
which this false World displays;
But give me lively Pow'r and Strength
to keep thy righteous Ways.

38 Confirm the Promise which thou mad'st,
and give thy Servant Aid,
Who to transgress thy sacred Laws
is awfully afraid.

39 The foul Disgrace I justly fear,
in Mercy, Lord, remove;
For all the Judgments thou ordain'st
are full of Grace and Love.

40 Thou know'st how after thy Commands
my longing Heart does pant:
O then make Haste to raise me up,
and promis'd Succour grant.

V A U.

41 Thy constant Blessing, Lord, bestow
to cheer my drooping Heart;
To me, according to thy Word,
thy saving Health impart.

42 So

42 So shall I, when my Foes upbraid,
   this ready Answer make:
   " In God I trust, who never will
   " his faithful Promise break."
43 Then let not quite the Word of Truth
   be from my Mouth remov'd;
   Since still my Ground of stedfast Hope
   thy just Decrees have prov'd.
44 So I to keep thy righteous Laws
   will all my Study bend;
   From Age to Age, my Time to come
   in their Observance spend.
45 Ere long I trust to walk at large,
   from all Incumbrance free;
   Since I resolve to make my Life
   with thy Commands agree.
46 Thy Laws shall be my constant Talk;
   and Princes shall attend,
   Whilst I the Justice of thy Ways
   with Confidence defend.
47 My longing Heart and ravish'd Soul
   shall both o'erflow with Joy,
   When in thy lov'd Commandments I
   my happy Hours employ.
48 Then will I to thy just Decrees
   lift up my willing Hands;
   My Care and Bus'nefs then shall be
   to study thy Commands.

Z A I N.

49 According to thy promis'd Grace,
   thy Favour, Lord, extend:
   Make good to me the Word, on which
   thy Servant's Hopes depend.
50 That only Comfort in Distress
   did all my Griefs control;
   Thy Word, when Troubles hemm'd me round,
   reviv'd my fainting Soul.
51 Insulting Foes did proudly mock,
   and all my Hopes deride;
   Yet, from thy Law, not all their Scoffs
   could make me turn aside.

52 Thy Judgments then, of antient Date,
　　I quickly call'd to Mind,
　Till, ravish'd with such Thoughts, my Soul
　　did speedy Comfort find.
53 Sometimes I stand amaz'd, like one
　　with deadly Horror struck,
　To think how all my sinful Foes
　　have thy just Laws forsook.
54 But I thy Statutes and Decrees
　　my cheerful Anthems made:
　Whilst thro' strange Lands and Deserts wild
　　I like a Pilgrim stray'd.
55 Thy Name, that cheer'd my Heart by Day,
　　has fill'd my Thoughts by Night;
　I then resolv'd by thy just Laws
　　to guide my Steps aright.
56 That Peace of Mind, which has my Soul
　　in deep Distress sustain'd,
　By strict Obedience to thy Will
　　I happily obtain'd.

CHETH.

57 O Lord, my God, my Portion Thou,
　　and sure Possession art;
　Thy Words I stedfastly resolve
　　to treasure in my Heart.
58 With all the Strength of warm Desires
　　I did thy Grace implore;
　Disclose, according to thy Word,
　　thy Mercy's boundless Store.
59 With due Reflection and strict Care
　　on all my Ways I thought;
　And so, reclaim'd to thy just Paths,
　　my wand'ring Steps I brought.
60 I lost no Time, but made great Haste,
　　resolv'd, without Delay,
　To watch that I might never more
　　from thy Commandments stray.
61 Tho' num'rous Troops of sinful Men
　　to rob me have combin'd;
　Yet I thy pure and righteous Laws
　　have ever kept in Mind.

62 In Dead of Night I will arise
  to sing thy solemn Praise:
  Convinc'd how much I always ought
  to love thy righteous Ways.
63 To such as fear thy holy Name
  myself I closely join;
  To all who their obedient Wills
  to thy Commands resign.
64 O'er all the Earth thy Mercy, Lord,
  abundantly is shed:
  O make me then exactly learn
  thy sacred Paths to tread.

TETH.

65 With me, thy Servant, Thou hast dealt
  most graciously, O Lord;
  Repeated Benefits bestow'd
  according to thy Word.
66 Teach me the sacred Skill by which
  right Judgment is attain'd,
  Who in Belief of thy Commands
  have stedfastly remain'd.
67 Before Affliction stopp'd my Course,
  my Footsteps went astray;
  But I have since been disciplin'd
  thy Precepts to obey.
68 Thou art, O Lord, supremely good,
  and all thou dost is so;
  On me thy Statutes to discern
  thy saving Skill bestow.
69 The Proud have forg'd malicious Lies
  my spotless Fame to stain;
  But my fix'd Heart, without Reserve,
  thy Precepts shall retain.
70 While pamper'd they, with prosp'rous Ills,
  in sensual Pleasures live,
  My Soul can relish no Delight
  but what thy Precepts give.
71 'Tis good for me that I have felt
  Affliction's chast'ning Rod,
  That I might duly learn and keep
  the Statutes of my God.

72 The Law that from thy Mouth proceeds,
of more Efteem I hold
Than untouch'd Mines, than thoufand Mines
of Silver and of Gold.

JOD.

73 To me, who am the Workmanfhip
of thy Almighty Hands,
The heav'nly Underftanding give
to learn thy juft Commands.
74 My Prefervation to thy Saints
ftrong Comfort will afford,
To fee Succefs attend my Hopes,
who trufted in thy Word.
75 That right thy Judgments are, I now
by fure Experience fee:
And that in Faithfulnefs, O Lord,
Thou haft afflicted me.
76 O let thy tender Mercy now
afford me needful Aid;
According to thy Promife, Lord,
to me thy Servant made.
77 To me thy faving Grace reftore,
that I again may live;
Whofe Soul can relifh no Delight,
but what thy Precepts give.
78 Defeat the Proud, who, unprovok'd,
to ruin me have fought,
Who only on thy facred Laws
employ my harmlefs Thought.
79 Let thofe that fear thy Name efpoufe
my Caufe, and thofe alone
Who have by ftrict and pious Search
thy facred Precepts known.
80 In thy blefs'd Statutes let my Heart
continue always found:
That Guilt and Shame, the Sinner's Lot,
may never me confound.

CAPH.

81 My Soul with long Expectance faints
to fee thy faving Grace;

Yet

PSALM cxix.

Yet still on thy unerring Word
  my Confidence I place.
82 My very Eyes consume and fail
  with waiting for thy Word:
  Oh! when wilt Thou thy kind Relief
  and promis'd Aid afford?
83 My Skin like shrivel'd Parchment shows,
  that long in Smoke is set;
  Yet no Affliction me can force
  thy Statutes to forget.
84 How many Days must I endure
  of Sorrow and Distress?
  When wilt Thou Judgment execute
  on them who me oppress?
85 The Proud have digg'd a Pit for me,
  that have no other Foes
  But such as are averse to Thee,
  and thy just Laws oppose.
86 With sacred Truth's eternal Laws
  all thy Commands agree.
  Men persecute me without Cause:
  Thou, Lord, my Helper be.
87 With close Designs against my Life
  they had almost prevail'd;
  But in Obedience to thy Will
  my Duty never fail'd.
88 Thy wonted Kindness, Lord, restore,
  my drooping Heart to cheer;
  That by thy righteous Statutes I
  my Life's whole Course may steer.

LAMED.

89 For ever and for ever, Lord,
  unchang'd Thou dost remain;
  Thy Word, establish'd in the Heav'ns,
  does all their Orbs sustain.
90 Thro' circling Ages, Lord, thy Truth
  immoveable shall stand,
  As doth the Earth, which thou uphold'st
  by thy Almighty Hand.
91 All Things the Course by Thee ordain'd
  ev'n to this Day fulfil:

They are thy faithful Subjects all,
  and Servants of thy Will.
92 Unless thy sacred Law had been
    my Comfort and Delight,
  I must have fainted, and expir'd
    in dark Affliction's Night.
93 Thy Precepts therefore from my Thoughts
    shall never, Lord, depart;
  For Thou by them hast to new Life
    restor'd my dying Heart.
94 As I am thine, entirely thine,
    protect me, Lord, from Harm;
  Who have thy Precepts sought to know,
    and carefully perform.
95 The Wicked have their Ambush laid,
    my guiltless Life to take;
  But in the Midst of Danger I
    thy Word my Study make.
96 I've seen an End of what we call
    Perfection here below:
  But thy Commandments, like Thyself,
    no Change or Period know.

M E M.

97 The Love that to thy Laws I bear
    no Language can display:
  They with fresh Wonders entertain
    my ravish'd Thoughts all Day.
98 Thro' thy Commands I wiser grow
    than all my subtle Foes;
  For thy sure Word doth me direct,
    and all my Ways dispose.
99 From me my former Teachers now
    may abler Counsel take:
  Because thy sacred Precepts I
    my constant Study make.
100 In Understanding I excel
    the Sages of our Days;
  Because by thy unerring Rules
    I order all my Ways.
101 My Feet with Care I have refrain'd
    from every sinful Way,

That

That to thy sacred Word I might
  entire Obedience pay.
102 I have not from thy Judgments stray'd,
  by vain Desires misled:
For, Lord, Thou hast instructed me
  thy righteous Paths to tread.
103 How sweet are all thy Words to me!
  O what divine Repast!
How much more grateful to my Soul
  than Honey to my Taste!
104 Taught by thy sacred Precepts, I
  with heav'nly Skill am blest;
Thro' which the treach'rous Ways of Sin
  I utterly detest.

N U N.

105 Thy Word is to my Feet a Lamp,
  the Way of Truth to show;
A Watch-light, to point out the Path
  in which I ought to go.
106 I swear (and from my solemn Oath
  I'll never start aside)
That in thy righteous Judgments I
  will stedfastly abide.
107 Since I with Griefs am so opprest,
  that I can bear no more;
According to thy Word, do Thou
  my fainting Soul restore.
108 Let still my Sacrifice of Praise
  with Thee Acceptance find;
And in thy righteous Judgments, Lord,
  instruct my willing Mind.
109 Tho' ghastly Dangers me surround,
  my Soul they cannot awe;
Nor with continual Terrors keep
  from thinking on thy Law.
110 My wicked and invet'rate Foes
  for me their Snares have laid:
Yet I have kept the upright Path,
  nor from thy Precepts stray'd.
111 Thy Testimonies I have made
  my Heritage and Choice;

For

For they, when other Comforts fail,
   my drooping Heart rejoice.
112 My Heart with early Zeal began
   thy Statutes to obey;
And, till my Courfe of Life is done,
   fhall keep thy upright Way.

SAMECH.

113 Deceitful Thoughts and Practices
   I utterly deteft;
But to thy Laws Affection bear
   too great to be expreft.
114 My Hiding-place, my Refuge-tower,
   and Shield, art Thou, O Lord;
I firmly anchor all my Hopes
   on thy unerring Word.
115 Hence, ye that trade in Wickednefs,
   approach not my Abode;
For firmly I refolve to keep
   the Precepts of my God.
116 According to thy gracious Word,
   from Danger fet me free;
Nor make me of thofe Hopes afham'd,
   that I repofe in Thee.
117 Uphold me; fo fhall I be fafe,
   and refcued from Diftrefs;
To thy Decrees continually
   my juft Refpect addrefs.
118 The Wicked Thou haft trod to Earth,
   who from thy Statutes ftray'd;
Their vile Deceit the juft Reward
   of their own Falfehood made.
119 The Wicked from thy holy Land
   Thou doft like Drofs remove;
I, therefore, with fuch Juftice charm'd,
   thy Teftimonies love.
120 Yet with that Love they make me dread,
   left I fhould fo offend,
When on Tranfgreffors I behold
   thy Judgments thus defcend.

AIN.

A I N.

121 Judgment and Justice I have lov'd;
  O therefore, Lord, engage
  In my Defence, nor give me up
  to my Oppressors' Rage.
122 Do Thou be Surety, Lord, for me:
  and so shall this Distress
  Prove good for me; nor shall the Proud
  my guiltless Soul oppress.
123 My Eyes, alas! begin to fail,
  in long Expectance held;
  Till thy Salvation they behold;
  and righteous Word fulfill'd.
124 To me, thy Servant in Distress,
  thy wonted Grace display,
  And discipline my willing Heart
  thy Statutes to obey.
125 On me, devoted to thy Fear,
  thy sacred Skill bestow;
  That of thy Testimonies I
  the full Extent may know.
126 'Tis Time, high Time, for Thee, O Lord,
  thy Vengeance to employ,
  When Men with open Violence
  thy sacred Law destroy.
127 Yet their Contempt of thy Commands
  but make their Value rise
  In my Esteem, who purest Gold
  compar'd with them despise.
128 Thy Precepts therefore I account,
  in all Respects, divine:
  They teach me to discern the right,
  and all false Ways decline.

P E.

129 The Wonders which thy Laws contain
  no Words can represent;
  Therefore to learn and practise them
  my zealous Heart is bent.
130 The very Entrance to thy Word
  celestial Light displays,

And Knowledge of true Happiness
to simplest Minds conveys.
131 With eager Hopes I waiting stood,
and fainted with Desire,
That of thy wise Commands I might
the sacred Skill acquire.
132 With Favour, Lord, look down on me,
who thy Relief implore;
As Thou art wont to visit those
that thy blest Name adore.
133 Directed by thy heavenly Word,
let all my Footsteps be;
Nor Wickedness of any Kind
Dominion have o'er me.
134 Release, entirely set me free.
from persecuting Hands,
That, unmolested, I may learn
and practise thy Commands.
135 On me, devoted to thy Fear,
Lord, make thy Face to shine:
Thy Statutes both to know and keep
my Heart with Zeal incline.
136 My Eyes to weeping Fountains turn,
whence briny Rivers flow,
To see Mankind against thy Laws
in bold Defiance go.

TSADDI.

137 Thou art the righteous Judge, in whom
wrong'd Innocence may trust;
And, like Thyself, thy Judgments, Lord,
in all Respects are just.
138 Most just and true those Statutes were,
which thou didst first decree;
And all with Faithfulness perform'd
succeeding Times shall see.
139 With Zeal my Flesh consumes away,
my Soul with Anguish frets,
To see my Foes contemn at once
thy Promises and Threats.
140 Yet each neglected Word of thine
(howe'er by them despis'd)

Is

  Is pure, and for eternal Truth
   by me thy Servant priz'd.
141 Brought, for thy Sake, to low Estate,
   Contempt from all I find;
  Yet no Affront or Wrongs can drive
   thy Precepts from my Mind.
142 Thy Righteousness shall then endure,
   when Time itself is past;
  Thy Law is Truth itself, that Truth
   which shall for ever last.
143 Tho' Trouble, Anguish, Doubts, and Dread,
   to compass me unite:
  Beset with Danger, still I make
   thy Precepts my Delight.
144 Eternal and unerring Rules
   thy Testimonies give:
  Teach me the Wisdom that will make
   my Soul for ever live.

K O P H.

145 With my whole Heart to God I call'd;
   Lord, hear my earnest Cry;
  And I thy Statutes to perform
   will all my Care apply.
146 Again more fervently I pray'd,
   O! save me, that I may
  Thy Testimonies throughly know,
   and stedfastly obey.
147 My earlier Prayer the dawning Day
   prevented, while I cry'd
  To Him, on whose engaging Word
   my Hope alone rely'd.
148 With Zeal have I awak'd before
   the Midnight Watch was set,
  That I of thy mysterious Word
   might perfect Knowledge get.
149 Lord, hear my supplicating Voice,
   and wonted Favour shew;
  O quicken me, and so approve
   thy Judgment ever true.
150 My persecuting Foes advance,
   and hourly nearer draw;
          What

What Treatment can I hope from them
  who violate thy Law?
151 Tho' they draw nigh, my Comfort is,
  Thou, Lord, art yet more near;
  Thou, whose Commands are righteous all,
  thy promises sincere.
152 Concerning thy divine Decrees,
  my Soul has known of old
  That they were true, and shall their Truth
  to endless Ages hold.

RESCH.

153 Consider my Affliction, Lord,
  and me from Bondage draw;
  Think on thy Servant in Distress,
  who ne'er forgets thy Law.
154 Plead Thou my Cause; to that and me
  thy timely Aid afford;
  With Beams of Mercy quicken me,
  according to thy Word.
155 From harden'd Sinners Thou remov'st
  Salvation far away:
  'Tis just Thou should'st withdraw from them,
  who from thy Statutes stray.
156 Since great thy tender Mercies are
  to all who Thee adore;
  According to thy Judgments, Lord,
  my fainting Hopes restore.
157 A num'rous Host of spiteful Foes
  against my Life combine;
  But all too few to force my Soul
  thy Statutes to decline.
158 Those bold Transgressors I beheld,
  and was with Grief oppress'd,
  To see with what audacious Pride
  thy Cov'nant they transgress'd.
159 Yet, while they slight, consider, Lord,
  how I thy Precepts love;
  Oh, therefore, quicken me with Beams
  of Mercy from above.
160 As from the Birth of Time thy Truth
  has held thro' Ages past,

So

So shall thy righteous Judgments, firm,
   to endless Ages last.

SCHIN.

161 Tho' mighty Tyrants, without Cause,
   conspire my Blood to shed,
   Thy sacred Word has Power alone
   to fill my Heart with Dread.
162 And yet that Word my joyful Breast
   with heavenly Rapture warms:
   Nor Conquest, nor the Spoils of War,
   have such transporting Charms.
163 Perfidious Practices and Lies
   I utterly detest;
   But to thy Laws Affection bear
   too vast to be express'd.
164 Seven Times a Day, with grateful Voice,
   thy Praises I resound,
   Because I find thy Judgments all
   with Truth and Justice crown'd.
165 Secure, substantial Peace have they
   who truly love thy Law;
   No smiling Mischief them can tempt,
   nor frowning Danger awe.
166 For thy Salvation I have hop'd,
   and, tho' so long delay'd,
   With cheerful Zeal and strictest Care
   all thy Commands obey'd.
167 Thy Testimonies I have kept,
   and constantly obey'd;
   Because the Love I bore to them
   thy Service easy made.
168 From strict Observance of thy Laws
   I never yet withdrew;
   Convinc'd that my most secret Ways
   are open to thy View.

TAU.

169 To my Request and earnest Cry
   attend, O gracious Lord;
   Inspire my Heart with heavenly Skill,
   according to thy Word.

170 Let

170 Let my repeated Pray'r at laſt
　　before thy Throne appear;
　　According to thy plighted Word
　　for my Relief draw near.
171 Then ſhall my grateful Lips return
　　the Tribute of their Praiſe,
　　When Thou thy Counſels haſt reveal'd,
　　and taught me thy juſt Ways.
172 My Tongue the Praiſes of thy Word
　　ſhall thankfully reſound,
　　Becauſe thy Promiſes are all
　　with Truth and Juſtice crown'd.
173 Let thy Almighty Arm appear,
　　and bring me timely Aid;
　　For I the Laws thou haſt ordain'd
　　my Heart's free Choice have made.
174 My Soul has waited long to ſee
　　thy ſaving Grace reſtor'd;
　　Nor Comfort knew, but what thy Laws,
　　thy heav'nly Laws afford.
175 Prolong my Life, that I may ſing
　　my great Reſtorer's Praiſe;
　　Whoſe Juſtice from the Depth of Woes
　　my fainting Soul ſhall raiſe.
176 Like ſome loſt Sheep I've ſtray'd, till I
　　deſpair my Way to find:
　　Thou, therefore, Lord, thy Servant ſeek,
　　who keeps thy Laws in Mind.

PSALM CXX.

1 IN deep Diſtreſs I oft have cry'd
　　To God, who never yet deny'd
　　To reſcue me oppreſs'd with Wrongs;
2 Once more, O Lord, Deliv'rance ſend,
　　From lying Lips my Soul defend,
　　And from the Rage of ſland'ring Tongues.
3 What little Profit can accrue,
　　And yet what heavy Wrath is due,
　　O thou perfidious Tongue, to thee!
4 Thy Sting upon thyſelf ſhall turn;
　　Of laſting Flames, that fiercely burn,
　　The conſtant Fuel thou ſhalt be.

5 But

5 But O! how wretched is my Doom,
  Who am a Sojourner become
    In barren *Mesech's* desert Soil!
  With *Kedar's* wicked Tents inclos'd,
  To lawless Savages expos'd,
    Who live on nought but Theft and Spoil.
6 My hapless Dwelling is with those
  Who Peace and Amity oppose,
    And Pleasure take in others'. Harms:
7 Sweet Peace is all I court and seek;
  But when to them of Peace I speak,
    They straight cry out, *To Arms, to Arms.*

PSALM CXXI.

1 TO *Sion's* Hill I lift my Eyes,
    from thence expecting Aid;
2 From *Sion's* Hill, and *Sion's* God,
    who Heav'n and Earth has made:
3 Then thou, my Soul, in Safety rest,
    thy Guardian will not sleep:
4 His watchful Care, that *Israel* guards,
    will *Israel's* Monarch keep.
5 Shelter'd beneath th' Almighty's Wings,
    thou shalt securely rest,
6 Where neither Sun nor Moon shall thee
    by Day or Night molest.
7 From common Accidents of Life
    his Care shall guard thee still;
  From the blind Strokes of Chance, and Foes
    that lie in wait to kill.
8 At Home, Abroad, in Peace, in War,
    thy God shall thee defend;
  Conduct thee thro' Life's Pilgrimage
    safe to thy Journey's End.

PSALM CXXII.

1 O 'twas a joyful Sound to hear
    our Tribes devoutly say,
  Up, *Israel*, to the Temple haste,
    and keep your Festal Day.
2 At *Salem's* Courts we must appear
    with our assembled Powers;

3 In strong and beauteous Order rang'd,
 like her united Towers.
4 'Tis thither, by divine Command,
 the Tribes of God repair,
 Before his Ark to celebrate
 his Name with Praise and Prayer.
5 Tribunals stand erected there,
 where Equity takes Place;
 There stand the Courts and Palaces
 of Royal *David's* Race.
6 O, pray we then for *Salem's* Peace,
 for they shall prosp'rous be,
 (Thou holy City of our God!)
 who bear true Love to Thee.
7 May Peace within thy sacred Walls
 a constant Guest be found;
 With Plenty and Prosperity
 thy Palaces be crown'd.
8 For my dear Brethren's Sake, and Friends,
 no less than Brethren dear,
 I'll pray—May Peace in *Salem's* Towers
 a constant Guest appear.
9 But most of all I'll seek thy Good,
 and ever wish thee well,
 For *Sion* and the Temple's Sake,
 where God vouchsafes to dwell.

PSALM CXXIII.

1, 2 ON Thee, who dwell'st above the Skies,
 For Mercy wait my longing Eyes;
 As Servants watch their Masters' Hands,
 And Maids their Mistresses' Commands.
3, 4 O then have Mercy on us, Lord;
 Thy gracious Aid to us afford:
 To us whom cruel Foes oppress,
 Grown rich and proud by our Distress.

PSALM CXXIV.

1 HAD not the Lord (may *Israel* say)
 been pleas'd to interpose,
2 Had he not then espous'd our Cause,
 when Men against us rose,

3, 4, 5 Their

3, 4, 5 Their Wrath had swallow'd us alive,
    and rag'd without Controul;
  Their Spite and Pride's united Floods
    had quite o'erwhelm'd our Soul.
6 But prais'd be our Eternal Lord,
    who rescued us that Day;
  Nor to their savage Jaws gave up
    our threaten'd Lives a Prey.
7 Our Soul is like a Bird escap'd
    from out the Fowler's Net;
  Their Snare is broke, their Hopes are cross'd,
    and we at Freedom set.
8 Secure in his Almighty Name,
    our Confidence remains,
  Who, as He made both Heaven and Earth,
    of both sole Monarch reigns.

PSALM CXXV.

1 WHO place on *Sion's* God their Trust,
    like *Sion's* Rock shall stand;
  Like her immoveable be fix'd
    by his Almighty Hand.
2 Look how the Hills on ev'ry Side
    Jerusalem inclose;
  So stands the Lord around his Saints,
    to guard them from their Foes.
3 The Wicked may afflict the Just,
    but ne'er too long oppress,
  Nor force him by Despair to seek
    base Means for his Redress.
4 Be good, O righteous God, to those
    who righteous Deeds affect:
  The Heart that Innocence retains,
    let Innocence protect.
5 All those who walk in crooked Paths
    the Lord shall soon destroy;
  Cut off th' Unjust, but crown the Saints
    with lasting Peace and Joy.

PSALM CXXVI.

1 WHEN *Sion's* God her Sons recall'd
    from long Captivity,

It seem'd at first a pleasing Dream
  of what we wish'd to see :
2 But soon, in unaccustom'd Mirth,
   we did our Voice employ,
 And sung our great Creator's Praise
   in thankful Hymns of Joy.
 Our Heathen Foes repining stood,
   yet were compell'd to own,
 That great and wondrous was the Work
   our God for us had done.
3 'Twas great, say they, 'twas wondrous great,
   much more should we confess ;
 The Lord has done great Things, whereof
   we reap the glad Success.
4 To us bring back the Remnant, Lord,
   of *Israel's* captive Bands,
 More welcome than refreshing Show'rs
   to parch'd and thirsty Lands.
5 That we, whose Work commenc'd in Tears,
   may see our Labours thrive,
 Till finish'd with Success, to make
   our drooping Hearts revive.
6 Tho' he despond that sows his Grain,
   yet doubtless he shall come
 To bind his full-ear'd Sheaves, and bring
   the joyful Harvest home.

PSALM CXXVII.

1 WE build with fruitless Cost, unless
    the Lord the Pile sustain ;
 Unless the Lord the City keep,
   the Watchman wakes in vain.
2 In vain we rise before the Day,
   and late to Rest repair ;
 Allow no Respite to our Toil,
   and eat the Bread of Care.
 Supplies of Life, with Ease to them,
   He on his Saints bestows ;
 He crowns their Labour with Success,
   their Nights with sound Repose.
3 Children, those Comforts of our Life,
   are Presents from the Lord ;

He

He gives a num'rous Race of Heirs,
  as Piety's Reward.
4 As Arrows in a Giant's Hand,
  when marching forth to War,
  Ev'n so the Sons of sprightly Youth
  their Parents Safeguard are.
5 Happy the Man, whose Quiver's fill'd
  with these prevailing Arms;
  He need not fear to meet his Foe
  at Law, or Warm's Alarms.

PSALM CXXVIII.

1 THE Man is blest that fears the Lord;
    not only Worship pays,
  But keeps his Steps confin'd with Care
    to his appointed Ways.
2 He shall upon the sweet Returns
    of his own Labour feed;
  Without Dependence live, and see
    his Wishes all succeed.
3 His Wife, like a fair fertile Vine,
    her lovely Fruit shall bring;
  His Children, like young Olive Plants,
    about his Table spring.
4, 5 Who fears the Lord, shall prosper thus;
    him *Sion's* God shall bless;
  And grant him all his Days to see
    Jerusalem's Success.
6 He shall live on, till Heirs from him
    descend with vast Increase;
  Much bless'd in his own prosp'rous State,
    and more in *Israel's* Peace.

PSALM CXXIX.

1 FROM my Youth up, may *Israel* say,
    they oft have me assail'd,
2 Reduc'd me oft to heavy Straits,
    but never quite prevail'd.
3 They oft have plough'd my patient Back
    with Furrows deep and long:
4 But our just God has broke their Chains,
    and rescued us from Wrong.

5 Defeat, Confusion, shameful Rout,
    be still the Doom of those,
  Their righteous Doom, who *Sion* hate,
    and *Sion's* God oppose.
6 Like Corn upon our Houses' Tops,
    untimely let them fade,
  Which too much Heat, and Want of Root,
    has blasted in the Blade:
7 Which in his Arms no Reaper takes,
    but unregarded leaves;
  Nor Binder thinks it worth his Pains
    to fold it into Sheaves.
8 No Traveller that passes by
    vouchsafes a Minute's Stop,
  To give it one kind Look, or crave
    Heaven's Blessing on the Crop.

PSALM CXXX.

1 FROM lowest Depths of Woe
    to God I send my Cry;
2 Lord, hear my supplicating Voice,
    and graciously reply.
3 Should'st Thou severely judge,
    who can the Trial bear?
4 But Thou forgiv'st, lest we despond,
    and quite renounce thy Fear.
5 My Soul with Patience waits
    for Thee, the living Lord;
  My Hopes are on thy Promise built,
    thy never-failing Word.
6 My longing Eyes look out
    for thy enlivening Ray,
  More duly than the Morning Watch
    to spy the dawning Day.
7 Let *Israel* trust in God,
    no Bounds his Mercy knows:
  The plenteous Source and Spring from whence
    eternal Succour flows.
8 Whose friendly Streams to us
    Supplies in Want convey:
  A healing Spring, a Spring to cleanse,
    and wash our Guilt away.

PSALM

PSALM CXXXI.

1 O Lord, I am not proud of Heart,
  nor cast a scornful Eye;
Nor my aspiring Thoughts employ
  in Things for me too high.
2 With infant Innocence, Thou know'st
  I have myself demean'd;
Compos'd to Quiet, like a Babe
  that from the Breast is wean'd.
3 Like me, let *Israel* hope in God,
  his Aid alone implore;
Both now and ever trust in him,
  who lives for evermore.

PSALM CXXXII.

1 LET *David*, Lord, a constant Place
  in thy Remembrance find;
Let all the Sorrows he endur'd
  be ever in thy Mind.
2 Remember what a solemn Oath
  to Thee, his Lord, he swore;
How to the mighty God he vow'd,
  whom *Jacob's* Sons adore:
3, 4 I will not go into my House,
  nor to my Bed ascend;
No soft Repose shall close my Eyes,
  nor Sleep my Eyelids bend;
5 Till for the Lord's design'd Abode
  I mark the destin'd Ground;
Till I a decent Place of Rest
  for *Jacob's* God have found.
6 Th' appointed Place, with Shouts of Joy,
  at *Ephrata* we found,
And made the Woods and neighb'ring Fields
  our glad Applause resound.
7 O with due Rev'rence let us then
  to his Abode repair;
And, prostrate at his Footstool fall'n,
  pour out our humble Pray'r.
8 Arise, O Lord, and now possess
  thy constant Place of Rest;

  Be that, not only with thy Ark,
   but with thy Presence blest.
9, 10 Clothe Thou thy Priests with Righteousness,
   make Thou thy Saints rejoice;
  And, for thy Servant *David's* Sake,
   hear thy Anointed's Voice.
11 God sware to *David* in his Truth,
   (nor shall his Oath be vain)
  One of thy Offspring after thee
   upon thy Throne shall reign:
12 And if thy Seed my Cov'nant keep,
   and to my Laws submit;
  Their Children too upon thy Throne
   for evermore shall sit.
13, 14 For *Sion* does in God's Esteem
   all other Seats excel;
  His Place of everlasting Rest,
   where He desires to dwell.
15, 16 Her Store, says He, I will increase,
   her Poor with Plenty bless;
  Her Saints shall shout for Joy, her Priests
   my saving Health confess.
17 There *David's* Pow'r shall long remain
   in his successive Line,
  And my anointed Servant there
   shall with fresh Lustre shine.
18 The Faces of his vanquish'd Foes
   Confusion shall o'erspread;
  Whilst with confirm'd Success his Crown
   shall flourish on his Head.

PSALM CXXXIII.

1 HOW vast must their Advantage be!
   how great their Pleasure prove!
  Who live like Brethren, and consent
   in Offices of Love:
2 True Love is like that precious Oil
   which, pour'd on *Aaron's* Head,
  Ran down his Beard, and o'er his Robes
   its costly Moisture shed.
3 'Tis like refreshing Dew, which does
   on *Hermon's* Top distil:

Or like the early Drops that fall
   on *Sion's* fruitful Hill.
4 For God to all, whose friendly Hearts
   with mutual Love abound,
Has firmly promis'd Length of Days
   with constant Blessings crown'd.

PSALM CXXXIV.

1 BLESS God, ye Servants that attend
   upon his solemn State;
That in his Temple, Night by Night,
   with humble Rev'rence wait:
2, 3 Within his House lift up your Hands,
   and bless his holy Name;
From *Sion* bless thy *Israel*, Lord,
   who Heav'n and Earth didst frame.

PSALM CXXXV.

1 O Praise the Lord with one Consent,
   and magnify his Name;
Let all the Servants of the Lord
   his worthy Praise proclaim.
2 Praise Him all ye that in his House
   attend with constant Care;
With those that to his outmost Courts
   with humble Zeal repair.
3 For this our truest Int'rest is,
   glad Hymns of Praise to sing;
And with loud Songs to bless his Name,
   a most delightful Thing.
4 For God his own peculiar Choice
   the Sons of *Jacob* makes;
And *Israel's* Offspring for his own
   most valued Treasure takes.
5 That God is great, we often have
   by glad Experience found;
And seen how He with wondrous Power
   above all Gods is crown'd.
6 For He with unresisted Strength
   performs his sov'reign Will;
In Heaven and Earth, and wat'ry Stores
   that Earth's deep Caverns fill.

7 He

7 He rises Vapours from the Ground,
    which, pois'd in liquid Air,
  Fall down at last in Show'rs, thro' which
    his dreadful Lightnings glare:
8 He from his Storehouse brings the Winds;
    and He with vengeful Hand
  The First-born slew of Man and Beast
    thro' *Egypt's* mourning Land.
9 He dreadful Signs and Wonders shew'd
    thro' stubborn *Egypt's* Coasts;
  Nor *Pharaoh* could his Plagues escape,
    nor all his num'rous Hosts.
10, 11 'Twas He that various Nations smote,
    and mighty Kings suppress'd;
  Sihon and *Og*, and all besides
    who *Canaan's* Land possess'd.
12, 13 Their Land upon his chosen Race
    He firmly did entail;
  For which his Fame shall always last,
    his Praise shall never fail.
14 For God shall soon his People's Cause
    with pitying Eyes survey;
  Repent Him of his Wrath, and turn
    his kindled Rage away.
15 Those Idols, whose false Worship spreads
    o'er all the Heathen Lands,
  Are made of Silver and of Gold,
    the Work of human Hands.
16, 17 They move not their fictitious Tongues,
    nor see with polish'd Eyes;
  Their counterfeited Ears are deaf,
    no Breath their Mouth supplies.
18 As senseless as themselves are they
    that all their Skill apply
  To make them, or in dang'rous Times
    on them for Aid rely.
19 Their just Returns of Thanks to God
    let grateful *Israel* pay;
  Nor let the Priests of *Aaron's* Race
    to bless the Lord delay.
20 Their Sense of his unbounded Love
    let *Levi's* House express;

And

PSALM cxxxv, cxxxvi.

And let all those that fear the Lord
his Name for ever bless.
21 Let all with Thanks his wondrous Works
in *Sion's* Courts proclaim;
Let them in *Salem*, where He dwells,
exalt his holy Name.

PSALM CXXXVI.

1 TO God the mighty Lord
   Your joyful Thanks repeat:
To Him due Praise afford,
As good as He is great.
   For God does prove
   Our constant Friend,
   His boundless Love
   Shall never end.

2, 3 To Him whose wondrous Power
All other Gods obey,
Whom earthly Kings adore,
This grateful Homage pay.
   For God, &c.

4, 5 By his Almighty Hand
Amazing Works are wrought;
The Heavens by his Command
Were to Perfection brought.
   For God, &c.

6 He spread the Ocean round
About the spacious Land;
And made the rising Ground
Above the Waters stand.
   For God, &c.

7, 8, 9 Thro' Heaven he did display
His num'rous Hosts of Light;
The Sun to rule by Day,
The Moon and Stars by Night.
   For God, &c.

10, 11, 12 He struck the First-born dead
Of *Egypt's* stubborn Land;
And thence his People led
With his resistless Hand.
   For God, &c.

13, 14 By

13, 14 By Him the raging Sea,
As if in Pieces rent,
Disclos'd a middle Way,
Thro' which his People went.
    For God, &c.

15 Where soon he overthrew
Proud *Pharaoh* and his Host,
Who, daring to pursue,
Were in the Billows lost.
    For God, &c.

16, 17, 18 Thro' Deserts vast and wild
He led the chosen Seed;
And famous Princes foil'd,
And made great Monarchs bleed.
    For God, &c.

19, 20 *Sihon*, whose potent Hand
Great *Ammon's* Sceptre sway'd;
And *Og*, whose stern Command
Rich *Bashan's* Land obey'd.
    For God, &c.

21, 22 And of his wondrous Grace,
Their Lands, whom he destroy'd,
He gave to *Israel's* Race,
To be by them enjoy'd.
    For God, &c.

23, 24 He in our Depth of Woes
On us with Favour thought,
And from our cruel Foes
In Peace and Safety brought.
    For God, &c.

25, 26 He does the Food supply,
On which all Creatures live:
To God who reigns on high
Eternal Praises give.
    For God will prove
    Our constant Friend,
    His boundless Love
    Shall never end.

PSALM CXXXVII.

1 WHEN we, our weary Limbs to rest,
Sat down by proud *Euphrates'* Stream,
    We

PSALM cxxxvii, cxxxviii.

We wept, with doleful Thoughts oppreſt,
And *Sion* was our mournful Theme.
2 Our Harps that, when with Joy we ſung,
Were wont their tuneful Parts to bear,
With ſilent Strings neglected hung
On Willow Trees that wither'd there.
3 Meanwhile our Foes, who all conſpir'd
To triumph in our ſlaviſh Wrongs,
Muſic and Mirth of us requir'd,
" Come, ſing us one of *Sion's* Songs."
4 How ſhall we tune our Voice to ſing?
Or touch our Harps with ſkilful Hands?
Shall Hymns of Joy to God our King
Be ſung by Slaves in foreign Lands?
5 O *Salem*, our once happy Seat!
When I of thee forgetful prove,
Let then my trembling Hand forget
The ſpeaking Strings with Art to move!
6 If I to mention thee forbear,
Eternal Silence ſeize my Tongue;
Or if I ſing one cheerful Air,
Till thy Deliv'rance is my Song.
7 Remember, Lord, how *Edom's* Race
In thy own City's fatal Day,
Cry'd out, " Her ſtately Walls deface,
" And with the Ground quite level lay."
8 Proud *Babel's* Daughter, doom'd to be
Of Grief and Woe the wretched Prey;
Bleſs'd is the Man who ſhall to thee
The Wrongs thou laid'ſt on us repay.
9 Thrice bleſs'd, who with juſt Rage poſſeſt,
And deaf to all the Parents Moans,
Shall ſnatch thy Infants from the Breaſt,
And daſh their Heads againſt the Stones.

PSALM CXXXVIII.

1 WITH my whole Heart, my God and King,
thy Praiſe I will proclaim;
Before the Gods with Joy I'll ſing,
and bleſs thy holy Name.
2 I'll worſhip at thy ſacred Seat;
and, with thy Love inſpir'd,

The

The Praises of thy Truth repeat,
  o'er all thy Works admir'd.
3 Thou graciously inclin'dst thine Ear,
  when I to Thee did cry;
And, when my Soul was press'd with Fear,
  didst inward Strength supply.
4 Therefore shall ev'ry earthly Prince
  thy Name with Praise pursue,
Whom these admir'd Events convince
  that all thy Works are true.
5 They all thy wondrous Ways, O Lord,
  with cheerful Songs shall bless;
And all thy glorious Acts record,
  thy awful Pow'r confess.
6 For God, altho' enthron'd on high,
  does thence the Poor respect,
The Proud far off his scornful Eye
  beholds with just Neglect.
7 Tho' I with Troubles am oppress'd,
  he shall my Foes disarm,
Relieve my Soul when most distress'd,
  and keep me safe from Harm.
8 The Lord, whose Mercies ever last,
  shall fix my happy State;
And, mindful of his Favours past,
  shall his own Work complete.

PSALM CXXXIX.

1,2 THOU, Lord, by strictest Search has known
    My rising up and lying down;
My secret Thoughts are known to Thee,
Known long before conceiv'd by me.
3 Thine Eye my Bed and Path surveys,
  My public Haunts and private Ways;
4 Thou know'st what 'tis my Lips would vent,
  My yet unutter'd Words Intent.
5 Surrounded by thy Pow'r I stand,
  On ev'ry Side I find thy Hand;
6 O Skill, for human Reach too high!
  Too dazzling bright for mortal Eye!
7 O could I so perfidious be,
  To think of once deserting Thee:

Where,

PSALM cxxxix.

Where, Lord, could I thy Influence shun?
Or whither from thy Presence run?
8 If up to Heaven I take my Flight,
'Tis there Thou dwell'st enthron'd in Light:
Or drive to Hell's infernal Plains,
'Tis there Almighty Vengeance reigns.
9 If I the Morning's Wings could gain,
And fly beyond the Western Main,
10 Thy swifter Hand would first arrive,
And there arrest the Fugitive.
11 Or should I try to shun thy Sight
Beneath the sable Wings of Night;
One Glance from Thee, one piercing Ray,
Would kindle Darkness into Day.
12 The Veil of Night is no Disguise,
No Screen from thy all-searching Eyes:
Thro' Midnight Shades Thou find'st thy Way,
As in the blazing Noon of Day.
13 Thou know'st the Texture of my Heart,
My Reins, and ev'ry vital Part,
Each single Thread, in Nature's Loom,
By Thee was cover'd in the Womb.
14 I'll praise Thee, from whose Hands I came,
A Work of such a curious Frame;
The Wonders Thou in me hast shown,
My Soul with grateful Joy must own.
15 Thine Eyes my Substance did survey,
While yet a lifeless Mass it lay;
In secret how exactly wrought,
Ere from its dark Inclosure brought.
16 Thou didst the shapeless Embryo see,
Its Parts were register'd by Thee:
Thou saw'st the daily Growth they took,
Form'd by the Model of thy Book.
17 Let me acknowledge too, O God,
That, since this Maze of Life I trod,
Thy Thoughts of Love to me surmount
The Pow'r of Numbers to recount.
18 Far sooner could I reckon o'er
The Sands upon the Ocean's Shore:
Each Morn revising what I've done,
I find th' Account but new begun.

19 The

19 The Wicked Thou shalt slay, O God:
  Depart from me, ye Men of Blood,
20 Whose Tongues Heaven's Majesty profane,
  And take th' Almighty's Name in vain.
21 Lord, hate not I their impious Crew,
  Who Thee with Enmity pursue?
  And does not Grief my Heart oppress,
  When Reprobates thy Laws transgress?
22 Who practise Enmity to Thee,
  Shall utmost Hatred have from me;
  Such Men I utterly detest,
  As if they were my Foes profess'd.
23, 24 Search, try, O God, my Thoughts and Heart,
  If Mischief lurks in any Part;
  Correct me where I go astray,
  And guide me in thy perfect Way.

PSALM CXL.

1 PReserve me, Lord, from crafty Foes
  of treacherous Intent;
2 And from the Sons of Violence,
  on open Mischief bent.
3 Their sland'ring Tongue the Serpent's Sting
  in Sharpness does exceed:
  Between their Lips the Gall of Asps
  and Adders' Venom breed.
4 Preserve me, Lord, from wicked Hands,
  nor leave my Soul forlorn;
  A Prey to Sons of Violence,
  who have my Ruin sworn.
5 The Proud for me have laid their Snare,
  and spread their wily Net;
  With Traps and Gins, where-e'er I move,
  I find myself beset.
6 But, thus environ'd with Distress,
  Thou art my God, I said;
  Lord, hear my supplicating Voice,
  that calls to Thee for Aid.
7 O Lord, the God whose saving Strength
  kind Succour did convey,
  And cover'd my advent'rous Head
  in Battle's doubtful Day;

8 Permit

8 Permit not their unjuft Defigns
    to anfwer their Defire;
    Left they, encourag'd by Succefs,
    to bolder Crimes afpire.
9 Let firft their Chiefs the fad Effects,
    of their Injuftice mourn;
    The Blaft of their envenom'd Breath
    upon themfelves return.
10 Let them who kindled firft the Flame,
    its Sacrifice become;
    The Pit they digg'd for me be made
    their own untimely Tomb.
11 Tho' Slander's Breath may raife a Storm,
    it quickly will decay;
    Their Rage doth but the Torrent fwell,
    that bears themfelves away.
12 God will affert the poor Man's Caufe,
    and fpeedy Succour give:
    The Juft fhall celebrate his Praife,
    and in his Prefence live.

PSALM CXLI.

1 TO thee, O Lord, my Cries afcend;
    O hafte to my Relief;
    And with accuftom'd Pity hear
    the Accents of my Grief.
2 Inftead of Off'rings, let my Prayer
    like Morning Incenfe rife;
    My lifted Hands fupply the Place
    of Evening Sacrifice.
3 From hafty Language curb my Tongue,
    and let a conftant Guard
    Still keep the Portal of my Lips,
    with wary Silence barr'd.
4 From wicked Men's Defigns and Deeds
    my Heart and Hands reftrain;
    Nor let me in the Booty fhare
    of their unrighteous Gain.
5 Let upright Men reprove my Faults,
    and I fhall think them kind;
    Like Balm that heals a wounded Head,
    I their Reproof fhall find;

    And, in Return, my fervent Prayer
       I shall for them address,
    When they are tempted and reduc'd,
       like me, to sore Distress.
6 When skulking in *Engedi's* Rock,
       I to their Chiefs appeal,
    If one reproachful Word I spoke,
       when I had Power to kill.
7 Yet us they persecute to Death;
       our scatter'd Ruins lie
    As thick as from the Hewer's Axe
       the sever'd Splinters fly.
8 But, Lord, to Thee I still direct
       my supplicating Eyes:
    Oh, leave not destitute my Soul,
       whose Trust on Thee relies.
9 Do Thou preserve me from the Snares
       that wicked Hands have laid;
    Let them in their own Nets be caught,
       while my Escape is made.

PSALM CXLII.

1 TO God with mournful Voice
       in deep Distress I pray'd;
2 Made Him the Umpire of my Cause,
       my Wrongs before him laid.
3 Thou didst my Steps direct,
       when my griev'd Soul despair'd;
    For, where I thought to walk secure,
       they had their Traps prepar'd.
4 I look'd, but found no Friend
       to own me in Distress;
    All Refuge fail'd, no Man vouchsaf'd
       his Pity or Redress.
5 To God at last I pray'd,
       Thou, Lord, my Refuge art;
    My Portion in the Land of Life,
       till Life itself depart.
6 Reduc'd to greatest Straits,
       to Thee I make my Moan;
    O save me from oppressing Foes,
       for me too pow'rful grown.

7 That I may praife thy Name,
   my Soul from Prifon bring;
   Whilft of thy kind Regard to me
   affembled Saints fhall fing.

PSALM CXLIII.

1 LORD, hear my Prayer, and to my Cry
     thy wonted Audience lend;
   In thy accuftom'd Faith and Truth
     a gracious Anfwer fend.
2 Nor at thy ftrict Tribunal bring
     thy Servant to be try'd;
   For in thy Sight no living Man
     can e'er be juftify'd.
3 The fpiteful Foe purfues my Life,
     whofe Comforts all are fled:
   He drives me into Caves as dark
     as Manfions of the Dead.
4 My Spirit therefore is o'erwhelm'd,
     and finks within my Breaft;
   My mournful Heart grows defolate,
     with heavy Woes oppreft.
5 I call to Mind the Days of old,
     and Wonders Thou haft wrought:
   My former Dangers and Efcapes
     employ my mufing Thought.
6 To Thee my Hands in humble Prayer
     I fervently ftretch out;
   My Soul for thy Refrefhment thirfts,
     like Land opprefs'd with Drought.
7 Hear me with Speed; my Spirit fails;
     thy Face no longer hide,
   Left I become forlorn, like them
     that in the Grave refide.
8 Thy Kindnefs early let me hear,
     whofe Truft on Thee depends;
   Teach me the Way where I fhould go;
     my Soul to Thee afcends.
9 Do Thou, O Lord, from all my Foes
     preferve and fet me free;
   A fafe Retreat againft their Rage
     my Soul implores from Thee.

10 Thou

10 Thou art my God, thy righteous Will
    inſtruct me to obey;
  Let thy good Spirit lead and keep
    my Soul in thy right Way.
11 Oh! for the Sake of thy great Name
    revive my drooping Heart:
  For thy Truth's Sake, to me diſtreſs'd
    thy promis'd Aid impart.
12 In Pity to my Suff'rings, Lord,
    reduce my Foes to Shame;
  Slay them that perſecute a Soul
    devoted to thy Name.

PSALM CXLIV.

1 FOR ever bleſs'd be God the Lord,
    Who does his needful Aid impart,
  At once both Strength and Skill afford
  To wield my Arms with warlike Art.
2 His Goodneſs is my Fort and Tower,
  My ſtrong Deliv'rance and my Shield;
  In Him I truſt, whoſe matchleſs Power
  Makes to my Sway fierce Nations yield.
3 Lord, what's in Man, that Thou ſhould'ſt love
  Such tender Care of Him to take?
  What in his Offspring could Thee move
  Such great Account of him to make?
4 The Life of Man does quickly fade,
  His Thoughts but empty are and vain,
  His Days are like a flying Shade,
  Of whoſe ſhort Stay no Signs remain.
5 In ſolemn State, O God, deſcend,
  Whilſt Heav'n its lofty Head inclines;
  The ſmoaking Hills aſunder rend,
  Of thy Approach the awful Signs.
6 Diſcharge thy dreadful Light'nings round,
  And make my ſcatter'd Foes retreat;
  Them with thy pointed Arrows wound,
  And their Deſtruction ſoon compleat.
7,8 Do Thou, O Lord, from Heav'n engage
  Thy boundleſs Pow'r my Foes to quell,
  And ſnatch me from the ſtormy Rage
  Of threat'ning Waves that proudly ſwell.

PSALM cxliv, cxlv.

Fight Thou againſt my foreign Foes,
Who utter Speeches falſe and vain;
Who, tho' in ſolemn Leagues they cloſe,
Their ſworn Engagements ne'er maintain.

9 So I to Thee, O King of Kings,
In joyful Hymns my Voice ſhall raiſe,
And Inſtruments of various Strings
Shall help me thus to ſing thy Praiſe.

10 " God does to Kings his Aid afford,
" To them his ſure Salvation ſends;
" 'Tis He that from the murd'ring Sword
" His Servant *David* ſtill defends."

11 Fight Thou againſt my foreign Foes,
Who utter Speeches falſe and vain;
Who, tho' in ſolemn Leagues they cloſe,
Their ſworn Engagements ne'er maintain.

12 Then our young Sons like Trees ſhall grow,
Well planted in ſome fruitful Place;
Our Daughters ſhall like Pillars ſhow,
Deſign'd ſome Royal Court to grace.

13 Our Garners, fill'd with various Store,
Shall us and ours with Plenty feed;
Our Sheep, increaſing more and more,
Shall Thouſands and Ten Thouſands breed.

14 Strong ſhall our lab'ring Oxen grow,
Nor in their conſtant Labour faint;
Whilſt we no War nor Slavery know,
And in our Streets hear no Complaint.

15 Thrice happy is that People's Caſe,
Whoſe various Bleſſings thus abound;
Who God's true Worſhip ſtill embrace,
And are with his Protection crown'd.

PSALM CXLV.

1, 2 THEE I'll extol, my God and King,
    thy endleſs Praiſe proclaim:
This Tribute daily I will bring,
    and ever bleſs thy Name.

3 Thou, Lord, beyond Compare art great,
    and highly to be prais'd;
Thy Majeſty, with boundleſs Height,
    above our Knowledge rais'd.

4 Renown'd for mighty Acts, thy Fame
  to future Times extends;
  From Age to Age thy glorious Name
  succeſſively deſcends.
5, 6 Whilſt I thy Glory and Renown,
  and wondrous Works expreſs,
  The World with me thy Might ſhall own,
  and thy great Pow'r confeſs.
7 The Praiſe that to thy Love belongs,
  they ſhall with Joy proclaim;
  Thy Truth, of all their grateful Songs,
  ſhall be the conſtant Theme.
8 The Lord is good; freſh Acts of Grace
  his Pity ſtill ſupplies;
  His Anger moves with ſloweſt Pace,
  his willing Mercy flies.
9, 10 Thy Love thro' Earth extends its Fame,
  to all thy Works expreſt;
  Theſe ſhew thy Praiſe, whilſt thy great Name
  is by thy Servants bleſt.
11 They, with the glorious Proſpect fir'd,
  ſhall of thy Kingdom ſpeak;
  And thy great Pow'r, by all admir'd,
  their lofty Subject make.
12 'God's glorious Works, of antient Date,
  ſhall thus to all be known;
  And thus his Kingdom's Royal State
  with public Splendor ſhown.
13 His ſtedfaſt Throne, from Changes free,
  ſhall ſtand for ever faſt;
  His boundleſs Sway no End ſhall ſee,
  but Time itſelf out-laſt.

PART II.

14, 15 The Lord doth them ſupport that fall,
  and makes the proſtrate riſe;
  For his kind Aid all Creatures call,
  who timely Food ſupplies.
16 Whate'er their various Wants require,
  with open Hand He gives;
  And ſo fulfils the juſt Deſire
  of ev'ry Thing that lives.

17, 18 How

PSALM cxlv, cxlvi.

17, 18 How holy is the Lord, how juſt!
how righteous all his Ways!
How nigh to him, who with firm Truſt
for his Aſſiſtance prays.
19 He grants the full Deſires of thoſe,
who Him with Fear adore;
And will their Troubles ſoon compoſe,
when they his Aid implore.
20 The Lord preſerves all thoſe with Care;
whom grateful Love employs:
But Sinners, who his Vengeance dare,
with furious Rage deſtroys.
21 My Time to come, in Praiſes ſpent,
ſhall ſtill advance his Fame;
And all Mankind, with one Conſent,
for ever bleſs his Name.

PSALM CXLVI.

1, 2 O Praiſe the Lord, and thou, my Soul,
for ever bleſs his Name:
His wondrous Love, while Life ſhall laſt,
my conſtant Praiſe ſhall claim.
3 On Kings, the greateſt Sons of Men,
let none for Aid rely;
They cannot ſave in dang'rous Times,
nor timely Help apply.
4 Depriv'd of Breath, to Duſt they turn,
and there neglected lie,
And all their Thoughts and vain Deſigns
together with them die.
5 Then happy he, who *Jacob's* God
for his Protector takes;
Who ſtill, with well-plac'd Hope, the Lord
his conſtant Refuge makes.
6 The Lord, who made both Heav'n and Earth
and all that they contain,
Will never quit his ſtedfaſt Truth,
nor make his Promiſe vain.
7 The Poor, oppreſt, from all their Wrongs
are eas'd by his Decree;
He gives th   needful Food,
and ſets t ⁣ ⁣Priſ'ners free.

8 By

8 By Him the Blind receive their Sight,
   the Weak and Fall'n he rears:
   With kind Regard and tender Love
   He for the Righteous cares.
9 The Strangers He preserves from Harm,
   the Orphan kindly treats,
   Defends the Widow, and the Wiles
   of wicked Men defeats.
10 The God that doth in *Sion* dwell
   is our eternal King:
   From Age to Age his Reign endures:
   let all his Praises sing.

PSALM CXLVII.

1 O Praise the Lord with Hymns of Joy,
    and celebrate his Fame!
   For pleasant, good, and comely 'tis
    to praise his holy Name.
2 His holy City God will build,
    tho' level'd with the Ground:
   Bring back his People, tho' dispers'd
    thro' all the Nations round.
3,4 He kindly heals the broken Hearts,
    and all their Wounds doth close;
   He tells the Number of the Stars,
    their sev'ral Names he knows.
5,6 Great is the Lord, and great his Pow'r,
    His Wisdom has no Bound;
   The Meek He raises, and throws down
    the Wicked to the Ground.
7 To God the Lord a Hymn of Praise
    with grateful Voices sing;
   To Songs of Triumph tune the Harp,
    and strike each warbling String.
8 He covers Heav'n with Clouds, and thence
    refreshing Rain bestows:
   Thro' Him on Mountain-tops the Grass
    with wondrous Plenty grows.
9 He savage Beasts, that loosely range,
    with timely Food supplies;
   He feeds the Ravens' tender Brood,
    and stops their hungry Cries.

PSALM cxlvii.

10 He values not the warlike Steed,
  but does his Strength difdain;
 The nimble Foot that fwiftly runs
  no Prize from Him can gain.
11 But He, to him that fears his Name,
  his tender Love extends:
 To him that on his boundlefs Grace
  with ftedfaft Hope depends.
12, 13 Let Sion and *Jerufalem*
  to God their Praife addrefs;
 Who fenc'd their Gates with maffy Bars,
  and does their Children blefs.
14, 15 Thro' all their Borders He gives Peace,
  with fineft Wheat they're fed;
 He fpeaks the Word, and what He wills
  is done as foon as faid.
16 Large Flakes of Snow, like fleecy Wool,
  defcend at his Command;
 And hoary Froft, like Afhes fpread,
  is fcatter'd o'er the Land.
17 When, join'd to thefe, he does his Hail
  in little Morfels break,
 Who can againft his piercing Cold
  fecure Defences make?
18 He fends his Word, which melts the Ice;
  He makes his Wind to blow,
 And foon the Streams, congeal'd before,
  in plenteous Currents flow.
19 By Him his Statutes and Decrees
  to *Jacob's* Sons were fhewn;
 And ftill to *Ifrael's* chofen Seed
  his righteous Laws are known.
20 No other Nation this can boaft,
  nor did He e'er afford
 To Heathen Lands his Oracles,
  and Knowledge of his Word.

Hallelujah.

PSALM CXLVIII.

1, 2 YE boundless Realms of Joy,
  Exalt your Maker's Fame;
His Praise your Song employ
 Above the starry Frame;
  Your Voices raise,
  Ye Cherubim
  And Seraphim,
  To sing his Praise.
3, 4 Thou Moon that rul'st the Night,
 And Sun that guid'st the Day,
Ye glitt'ring Stars of Light,
 To Him your Homage pay;
  His Praise declare,
  Ye Heavens above,
  And Clouds that move
  In liquid Air.
5, 6 Let them adore the Lord,
 And praise his holy Name,
By whose Almighty Word
 They all from Nothing came;
  And all shall last
  From Changes free:
  His firm Decree
  Stands ever fast.
7, 8 Let Earth her Tribute pay;
 Praise Him, ye dreadful Whales,
And Fish that thro' the Sea
 Glide swift with glitt'ring Scales;
  Fire, Hail, and Snow,
  And misty Air,
  And Winds that, where
  He bids them, blow.
9, 10 By Hills and Mountains (all
 In grateful Concert join'd);
By Cedars stately tall,
 And Trees for Fruit design'd;
  By every Beast,
  And creeping Thing,
  And Fowl of Wing,
  His Name be blest.

       11, 12 Let

PSALM cxlviii, cxlix.

11, 12 Let all of Royal Birth,
    With those of humbler Frame,
And Judges of the Earth,
    His matchless Praise proclaim.
      In this Design
      Let Youths with Maids,
      And hoary Heads
      With Children join.

13 United Zeal be shewn,
    His wondrous Fame to raise,
Whose glorious Name alone
    Deserves our endless Praise.
      Earth's utmost Ends
      His Pow'r obey:
      His glorious Sway
      The Sky transcends.

14 His chosen Saints to grace,
    He sets them up on high,
And favours *Israel's* Race,
    Who still to him are nigh.
      O therefore raise
      Your grateful Voice,
      And still rejoice
      The Lord to praise.

PSALM CXLIX.

1, 2 O Praise ye the Lord,
    prepare your glad Voice,
His Praise in the great
    Assembly to sing;
In our great Creator
    let *Israel* rejoice,
And Children of *Sion*
    Be glad in their King.

3, 4 Let them his great Name
    extol in the Dance;
With Timbrel and Harp
    his Praises express;
Who always takes Pleasure
    his Saints to advance,
And with his Salvation
    the Humble to bless.

5, 6 With Glory adorn'd
    his People shall sing
To God, who their Beds
    with Safety does shield;
Their Mouths fill'd with Praises
    of Him their great King;
Whilst a two-edged Sword
    their Right-hand shall wield.

7, 8 Just Vengeance to take
    for Injuries past;
To punish those Lands
    for Ruin design'd;
With Chains, as their Captives,
    to tie their Kings fast,
With Fetters of Iron
    their Nobles to bind.

9 Thus shall they make good,
    when them they destroy,
The dreadful Decree
    which God does proclaim:
Such Honour and Triumph
    his Saints shall enjoy:
O therefore for ever
    exalt his great Name.

PSALM CL.

1 O Praise the Lord in that blest Place
    from whence his Goodness largely flows:
Praise Him in Heaven, where He his Face
    unveil'd in perfect Glory shows.

2 Praise Him for all the mighty Acts,
    which He in our Behalf has done;
His Kindness this Return exacts,
    with which our Praise should equal run.

3 Let the shrill Trumpet's warlike Voice
    make Rocks and Hills his Praise rebound;
Praise Him with Harp's melodious Noise,
    and gentle Psalt'ry's silver Sound.

4 Let Virgin Troops soft Timbrels bring,
    and some with graceful Motion dance;
Let Instruments of various Strings,
    with Organs join'd, his Praise advance.

PSALM cl.

5 Let them, who joyful Hymns compose,
    to Cymbals set their Songs of Praise;
Cymbals of common Use, and those
    that loudly sound on solemn Days.
6 Let all that vital Breath enjoy,
    the Breath He does to them afford
In just Returns of Praise employ:
    let ev'ry Creature praise the Lord.

GLORIA PATRI, &c.

Common Measure.

TO Father, Son, and Holy Ghost,
    the God whom we adore,
Be Glory, as it was, is now,
    and shall be evermore.

As Psalm 25.

To God the Father, Son,
    and Spirit, Glory be;
As 'twas, and is, and shall be so
    to all Eternity.

As the 100th Psalm.

To Father, Son, and Holy Ghost,
    the God whom Heav'n and Earth adore,
Be Glory, as it was of old,
    is now, and shall be evermore.

As Psalm 112, and the last Part of the 113th Psalm Tune.

To Father, Son, and Holy Ghost,
The God whom Heav'n's triumphant Host
    and suff'ring Saints on Earth adore,
Be Glory, as in Ages past,
As now it is, and so shall last,
    when Time itself must be no more.

As Psalm 148.

To God the Father, Son,
    And Spirit ever bless'd,
Eternal Three in One,
All Worship be address'd,
    As heretofore
It was, is now,
And shall be so
For evermore.

As Psalm 149.

By Angels in Heav'n
    of ev'ry Degree,
And Saints upon Earth,
    all Praise be address'd
To God in Three Persons,
    One God ever bless'd;
As it has been, now is,
    and always shall be.

HYMNS.

VENI CREATOR.

[Second Metre.]

COME, Holy Ghost; Creator, come;
   inspire the Souls of thine,
Till ev'ry Heart which Thou hast made
   is fill'd with Grace Divine.
Thou art the Comforter, the Gift
   of God, and Fire of Love;
The everlasting Spring of Joy,
   and Unction from above.
Thy Gifts are manifold; Thou writ'st
   God's Laws in each true Heart;
The Promise of the Father, Thou
   dost heav'nly Speech impart.
Enlighten our dark Souls, till they
   thy sacred Love embrace;
Assist our Minds, by Nature frail,
   with thy celestial Grace.
Drive far from us the mortal Foe,
   and give us Peace within;
That, by thy Guidance bless'd, we may
   escape the Snares of Sin.
Teach us the Father to confess,
   and Son from Death reviv'd;
And with them both, thee, Holy Ghost,
   who art from both deriv'd.
With Thee, O Father, therefore may
   the Son from Death restor'd,
And sacred Comforter, one God,
   devoutly be ador'd:
As in all Ages heretofore
   has constantly been done,
As now it is, and shall be so,
   when Time his Course has run.

SONG

SONG of the ANGELS at the Nativity of
our Blessed SAVIOUR.

Luke II. from Ver. 8, to Ver. 15.

WHILE Shepherds watch'd their Flocks by
    all seated on the Ground, [Night,
The Angel of the Lord came down,
  and Glory shone around.

" Fear not," said he, (for mighty Dread
  had seiz'd their troubled Mind);
" Glad Tidings of great Joy I bring
  " to you, and all Mankind.

" To you, in David's Town, this Day
  " is born, of David's Line,
" The Saviour, who is Christ the Lord;
  " and this shall be the Sign:

" The heav'nly Babe you there shall find
  " to human View display'd,
" All meanly wrapt in Swathing-bands,
  " and in a Manger laid."

Thus spake the Seraph, and forthwith
  appear a shining Throng
Of Angels, praising God, and thus
  address their joyful Song:

" All Glory be to God on high,
  " and to the Earth be Peace;
" Good-will, henceforth, from Heav'n to Men
  " begin and never cease."

For EASTER-DAY.

[First Hymn.]

* SINCE Christ, our Passover, is slain
    a Sacrifice for all;
Let all with thankful Hearts agree
    to keep the Festival;

Not with the Leaven, as of old,
    of Sin and Malice fed;
But with unfeign'd Sincerity,
    and Truth's unleaven'd Bread.

† Christ, being rais'd by Pow'r Divine,
    and rescued from the Grave,
Shall die no more, Death shall on him
    no more Dominion have.

‡ For that He dy'd, 'twas for our Sins
    He once vouchsaf'd to die:
But that he lives, he lives to God
    for all Eternity.

‖ So count yourselves as dead to Sin,
    but graciously restor'd,
And made, henceforth, alive to God
    through Jesus Christ our Lord.

To Father, Son, and Holy Ghost,
    the God whom we adore,
Be Glory, as it was, is now,
    and shall be evermore.

* 1 Cor. v. 7.   † Rom. vi. 9.   ‡ Ib. v. 10.   ‖ Ib. v. 11.

For EASTER-DAY.

[Second Hymn.]

* CHRIST from the Dead is rais'd, and made
    the First-fruits of the Tomb;
For as by Man came Death, by Man
    did Resurrection come.

† For as in *Adam* all Mankind
    did Guilt and Death derive,
So by the Righteousness of Christ
    shall all be made alive.

‡ If then ye risen are with Christ,
    seek only how to get
The Things that are above, where Christ
    at God's Right-hand is set.

To Father, Son, and Holy Ghost,
    The God whom we adore,
Be Glory, as it was, is now,
    and shall be evermore.

* 1 Cor. xv. 20, 21.   † Ibid.   ‡ Col. iii. 1.

AN ALPHABETICAL TABLE,

Shewing how to find any PSALM by its Beginning.

Pfalm A.	Page
AGainft all thofe	47
As pants the Hart	60
At length by certain	101
B.	
Behold, O God	115
Blefs God, my Soul	148
Blefs God, ye Servants	201
D.	
Defend me, Lord	40
Deliver me, O Lord	81
Do Thou, O God	77
F.	
For ever blefs'd	212
For Thee, O God	87
From loweft Depths	198
From my Youth up	197
G.	
Give Ear, thou Judge	75
God in the great	120
God is our Refuge	66
God's Temple crowns	126
H.	
Had not the Lord	194
Happy the Man	59
Have Mercy, Lord	72
Hear, O my People	109
He's blefs'd whofe Sins	43
He that has God	133
Hold not thy Peace	120
How blefs'd are they	174
How blefs'd is he	3
How good and pleafant	134
How long wilt Thou	16
How num'rous, Lord	5
How vaft muft their	200
J.	
Jehovah reigns, let all	140
Jehovah reigns, let theref.	142
I'll celebrate thy Praifes	39

Pfalm	Page
In deep Diftrefs	192
In Judah the	106
In Thee I put	97
In vain, O lawlefs Man	73
Judge me, O lord	35
Juft Judge of Heav'n	61
I waited meekly	57
L.	
Let all the Juft	44
Let all the Lands	88
Let all the lift'ning	68
Let David, Lord	199
Let God, the God	90
Lord, hear my Cry	83
Lord, hear my Pray'r	211
Lord, hear the Voice	6
Lord, hear the Voice	86
Lord, let thy juft	99
Lord, not to us	169
Lord, fave me for	75
Lord, Thou haft granted	123
Lord, who's the happy	17
M.	
My crafty Foe with	50
My God, my God, why	29
My Soul for Help	84
My Soul infpir'd	146
My Soul with grateful	171
N.	
No Change of Times	20
O.	
O all ye People	66
O come, loud Anthems	138
Of Mercy's never	143
O God, my gracious	85
O God, my Heart	162
O God of Hofts	122
O God, to whom	136
O God, who haft	82
O God, whofe former	163
O Ifrael's	

An Alphabetical Table, &c.

Psalm	Page
O Israel's Shepherd	116
O Lord, I am not	199
O Lord, my God	8
O Lord, my Rock	38
O Lord, our Fathers	62
O Lord, the Saviour	131
O Lord, thou art my	5
O Lord, to my	96
On Thee who dwell'st	194
O praise the Lord, for	172
O praise the Lord, and	215
O praise the Lord, in	220
O praise the Lord with	216
O praise the Lord with one	201
O praise ye the Lord	219
O render Thanks, and	151
O render Thanks to	154
O Thou, to whom all	10
O 'twas a joyful	193

P.

Praise ye the Lord	166
Preserve me, Lord	208
Protect me from my	18

R.

Resolv'd to watch	56

S.

Save me, O God	94
Since godly Men	15
Since I have plac'd	14
Sing to the Lord	159
Sing to the Lord	141
Speak, O ye Judges	80
Sure, wicked Fools	16

T.

Thee I'll extol	213
The Heav'ns declare	25
The King, O Lord	27
The Lord hath spoke	70
The Lord Himself	32
The Lord, the only God	67
The Lord to thy Request	26
The Lord unto my Lord	166
The Man is blest who fears	197

Psalm	Page
That Man is blest, who	167
The wicked Fool's	74
This spacious Earth	32
Tho' wicked Men	51
Thou, Lord, by strictest	206
Through all the changing	45
Thy chast'ning Wrath	54
Thy dreadful Anger	7
Thy Mercy, Lord	79
Thy Mercies, Lord	128
Thy Presence why	12
To bless thy chosen	90
To celebrate thy Praise	10
To God I cry'd	107
To God in whom	33
To God our never	118
To God the mighty	203
To God with mournful	210
To God your grateful	158
To my Complaint	124
To my just Plea	19
To Thee, my God	126
To Thee, O God	105
To Thee, O Lord	209
To Sion's Hill	193

W.

We build with	196
When I pour out	144
When Israel by	163
When Sion's God	195
When we our weary	204
While I the King's	64
Whom shall I fear	36
Who place on Sion's God	195
Why hast Thou cast	103
With cheerful Notes	172
With Glory clad	135
With my whole Heart	205
With one Consent	143
With restless and	3

Y.

Ye boundless Realms	218
Ye Princes that	39
Ye Saints and Servants	168

DIRECTIONS

DIRECTIONS

ABOUT THE

TUNES and MEASURES.

ALL Pfalms of this Verfion in the *common* Meafures of Eights and Sixes, (that is, where the firſt and third Lines of the ſingle Stanza conſiſt of eight Syllables each, the ſecond and fourth Lines of ſix Syllables each) may be ſung to any of the moſt uſual Tunes, *viz. York*-Tune, *Windſor*-Tune, St. *David's, Lichfield, Canterbury, Martyrs, Southwell,* St. *Mary's,* alias *Hackney*-Tune, &c.

As the Old 25th Pſalm, may be ſung the New 25, 31, 67, 130.

As the Old 113th, the 37, 46, 50, 63, 76, 91, 100, 113, 120.

As the Old 148th, the 136, 140.

As the Old 104th, the 149th.

The Pſalms in this Verſion of four Lines in a ſingle Stanza, and eight Syllables in each Line (if Pſalms of Praiſe or Cheerfulneſs) may properly be ſung as the Old 100th Pſalm, or to the Tune of the Old 125th Pſalm, Second Metre.

The Penitential or Mournful Pſalms, in the ſame Meaſure, may be ſung as the Old 51ſt Pſalm.

FINIS.

www.ingramcontent.com/pod-product-compliance
Lightning Source LLC
Chambersburg PA
CBHW021828230426
43669CB00008B/898